OH, MIND
RELAX PLEASE !
ROOTS OF YOGA
WINGS OF MANAGEMENT

SWAMI
SUKHABODHANANDA
Author of all time best seller
Oh, LIFE RELAX PLEASE!

authorHOUSE™

1663 Liberty Drive, Suite 200
Bloomington, Indiana 47403
(800) 839-8640
www.AuthorHouse.com

First published by AuthorHouse 07/21/05

ISBN: 1-4184-7420-7 (e)
ISBN: 1-4184-4271-2 (sc)

Printed in the United States of America
Bloomington, Indiana

This book is printed on acid-free paper.

Published by Prasanna Trust
300/18, 6th Main, 14th Cross, Vyalikaval
Bangalore 560 003, India

Year of publication : January 2002

First Edition   –   No. of copies : 5,000
Second Edition   –   No. of copies : 3,000
Third Edition   –   No. of copies : 3,000
Fourth Edition   –   No. of copies : 5,000
Fifth Edition   –   No. of copies : 5,000
Sixth Edition   –   No. of copies : 5,000
Seventh Edition –   No. of copies : 5,000
Eighth Edition   –   No. of copies : 5,000

Cover Design : Suresh UT

Book Layout : Govardhan Kini K

Printed at
SUDHINDRA
Malleswaram, Bangalore 560 003

Price :

REFLECTION

If you serve the universe;

the universe will serve you.

Reflect on this incident: -

Fleming, a poor Scottish farmer, heard a cry for help. A boy mired to his waist in black muck was struggling to free himself. Fleming saved the boy.

Next day, an elegantly dressed nobleman came to Fleming & said, "You have saved my son. I want to reward you for your act'.

"No, I cannot accept any reward for my act. It was my duty,' replied Fleming.

"Is that your son?' the nobleman asked pointing to the lad standing next. Fleming nodded in affirmation.

The nobleman offered to educate Fleming's son as a goodwill gesture. "Your son will make you proud' was his assurance.

Years passed. Fleming's son went on to become Sir Alexander Fleming, who discovered Penicillin. Years later, the nobleman's son was stricken with deadly pneumonia. What saved him? "Penicillin vaccine.'

The name of the nobleman was Lord Randolph Churchill. His son was Sir Winston Churchill.

Someone said, what goes around comes around.

There are two types of actions; outer & inner. What determines the quality of one's life is the inner action – thoughts and emotions. Be alert to every moment in your thoughts & emotions and learn to relax.

As you read this book, you will be sensitive to your thoughts and emotions. Observe the gaps between the thoughts and emotions. It is in these gaps your life will start flowering and relaxing.

Gift this book to your friends and relatives; let the law of grace emerge and lead you to inner peace.

With blessings,

SWAMI SUKHABODHANANDA

FROM THE AUTHOR

I have always told myself if I cannot be happy here and now, I will never be happy anywhere. This book is an offering of my happiness.

The superficial way of reading this book is through intellectual understanding. The deeper way is by feeling the insights of the narration. The deepest way is where these insights and parables light up your mind in your hours of darkness and guide you like a friend.

Hence my invitation is to read this book not just once, but many times over like a daily prayer....... for prayer is not changing the Lord but changing you.

By ingesting the essence of this book, you will realise what lies before you and behind you are nothing in comparison to what lies within you. Enlightenment is looking for spectacles that are sitting right on your nose. This book is about awakening you.... like a wake up call.

To do what you like and like what you do is indeed a divine work. Work is an opportunity to find oneself. This book helps you in finding yourself in all walks of life... intimate, family, work, social, and spiritual zones. In the process, you will be grateful to the weeds of your mind. They ultimately help your practice of being relaxed.

Being relaxed is wise. Begin with being wise and you will be relaxed. Being relaxed is a wise and an easy way to live life.

Life, thus lived will bring forth the peace of a rose garden and light of the luminous Sun as a part of your being.

Let your growth bring the best seasons of your life. This is my humble prayer for you.

I specially thank P. R. Madhav for editing this book. My special thanks to Mrs. Devki Jaipuria for all her support. My salutation to my loving mother who is a living Goddess. My deepest gratitude to all my Gurus for whom I have no words to express. I offer this book to all my students who are like little lamps shining in the night, which the great Sun cannot do. This is my dream and I am sure you will join me in making it as your destination.

With blessings,

SWAMI SUKHABODHANANDA

FOREWORD

"Losing is victory postponed'

"World will forgive failures, but will not forgive people who have not utilised the opportunities'.

This book contains many more such thought provoking maxims. Swamiji presents complex Vedantic truths in a simple manner like a sugarcoated pill. The name Oh, Mind Relax Please! itself creates curiosity among the readers.

This book blends the truths expounded by Allah, Krishna, Christ, Buddha, Mahaveera ….. and gives many insights to the readers.

This book provides solace and counsel to people who run away from the day-to-day problems of life. Swamiji's teaching guides one not to be upset with the problem; instead take problem as a challenge and solve it energetically.

This book is unique in its presentation where narrations are real life instances in the form of parables which touches the readers' heart. Besides, this book can be read from any chapter, but still it will stimulate the reader – like a pealed banana, which can be eaten from any side, thus enjoying its sweetness.

Every insight presented in this book teaches us how valuable our life is. If one digests and uses the rich wisdom, one will attain peace in life.

CHIRANJEEVI
The Mega Star

*Our heartfelt thanks to all enlightened masters &
modern thinkers for their inspirational guidance.*

Table of Contents

SUCH IS THE WAY

I have noticed that people the world over raise the same question when in distress. Their language may vary, but their question is the same, "Why does God burden only me with so much strife?"

When someone asks me this question, I tell them a short story from the Buddhist lore.

There was a small village. A young boy from the village was playing on the banks of a nearby river one evening. As he was playing, he heard a cry, "Oh, save me; some one please save me!"

Looking around, he found a crocodile caught in a net; unable to escape, the crocodile was crying out pitifully. The boy was reluctant to save the crocodile, fearing that if he saved it, the crocodile would make a meal of him. But the crocodile continued to plead with him, tears streaming down its face, and saying, "Honestly, I promise you I won't harm you. Please save me!"

The boy, convinced of its sincerity, began to cut the net that held the crocodile. No sooner was its head free from the net than did the crocodile grab the boy's leg in its jaws.

Now it was the boy's turn to cry for help. He said, "Hey, you dirty croc! Is this fair?" The crocodile responded philosophically, "What shall I do? Such is the way of the world! Such is life!", and began to drag the boy bit by bit into deeper water.

The boy was worried about dying. But what upset him more were the crocodile's total ingratitude and its philosophy.

As his leg was slowly sliding into the jaws of the crocodile, the boy saw some birds resting on a nearby tree and asked them, "Is the crocodile telling the truth? Is ingratitude the way of the world? Is this how life goes on? Are words not honored in this world?"

The birds replied, "We take such care to build safe nests on tree tops to protect our eggs. Yet, snakes come and swallow them. We agree with the crocodile. What it is saying is totally true. The world is essentially unjust and ungrateful."

Then the boy saw a donkey that was grazing on the banks of the lake and repeated his question. The donkey replied,

"When I was young, my master loaded soiled clothes on my back and extracted maximum work from me. Now that I am old and feeble, he has abandoned me saying that he cannot feed me. So there is nothing wrong with what the crocodile is saying. Such is the way of the world. The world is rife with injustice and ingratitude."

The boy still refused to accept these explanations. He saw a rabbit and repeated his question. The rabbit said, "No, no! I do not accept what the crocodile is saying. It is utter nonsense!"

Hearing this, the crocodile became angry and wanted to argue with the rabbit, even while holding the boy's leg in its jaws. The rabbit protested, saying that as the crocodile's mouth was choked with the boy's leg, it was not able to make out what the crocodile was trying to say. The crocodile laughed heartily at this and said, "I am not a fool! If I let go of his leg, the boy will run away!"

"Now, you are really stupid!" said the rabbit. "Have you forgotten how strong your tail is? Even if he runs, you can smash him with just one mighty lash of your tail!"

The crocodile fell for this, and releasing the boy, continued its argument. The rabbit shouted to the boy, "Run! Run! Don't just stand there!" and the boy took to his heels.

Only when it tried to raise its tail did the crocodile realize that it was still entangled in the net. As the boy ran away, it glared at the rabbit in terrible rage.

The rabbit smiled sweetly and quipped, "Now, do you understand? Such is the way of the world! Such is life!"

In a short while, the young boy returned with people from the village and they killed the crocodile. Meanwhile, a dog that came along spotted the rabbit and started chasing it. The boy screamed at the dog, "Hey, listen! That rabbit saved my life. Don't harm him." But alas, before the boy could intervene, the dog had chased and killed the rabbit!

The young boy, overcome by sadness, cried and said to himself, "What the crocodile said was true. Such is the way of the world. Such is life!"

Buddhism speaks of the same great truth that the ancient sages of Hinduism revealed – we cannot fully understand the many sides of reality that constitute our lives.

Unfairness is a part and parcel of life. That is the way of the world. Can we teach ourselves not to be victims of unfairness? Can we come to terms with the understanding that the mysteries of life cannot be fully comprehended?

An acceptance of the pervasiveness of unfairness would give us the maturity to live wisely.

Reflections

Yoga of Wisdom

*Watch – Mystery of Life is beyond our Comprehension.
We are mysteriously complete.*

Yoga of Action

*There is far more peace in acceptance
than in resistance*

Contemplation

Unfairness is a part and parcel of life.

A crocodile remains a crocodile even if dressed in silk.

He that kills shall be killed. He that cheats shall be cheated.

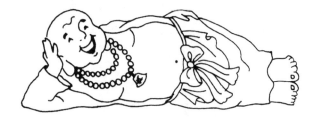

SECRETS OF PARENTING

The serene atmosphere of the Ashram complements the beauty around it. It is very pleasant to be in the Ashram. One mother, however, is agitated. The tranquility of the Ashram has no impact on her. She expresses her concerns about bringing up her children in this world. How is she going to keep them away from drugs, alcohol, and the attractions of sexuality?

Her words betray her fear and pain, "Swamiji, I become miserable when I think of my children in this wicked world. How can I bring them up so that they are not tainted?"

Often I go to the very roots of such fears. When we operate out of fear, we transmit the energy of fear to our children, in however subtle a way. If we were to operate out of trust, we would transmit trust to our children.

We have to realize that our actions are born out of our thoughts. Our thoughts are the products of our values, and values come from our own belief system. If we believe life is miserable, we attract misery; if we believe life is beautiful, we attract happiness. This is called the Law of Attraction.

We get what we focus on; so focus on good things so that only good would happen to our children. This is one of the variables that affect our children strongly.

The mother asks again, "Why do children detest advice?"

My question is, "Are they really against advice or against the way we administer it?" Every parent should be sensitive to this aspect.

Reflect on this story:

A money-minded son, after having his lunch, wrote a note to his mother saying that she owed him $25. He gave a detailed account - $ 5 for cleaning the house, $5 for washing the dishes, $15 for mowing the lawn. The mother was shocked by the note. She, however decided to educate her son.

She wrote a note and kept it on the dinning table. The note read, "Dear son, you owe me nothing." My account runs like this:

$ 0 for cooking your food

$ 0 for washing your clothes

$ 0 for ironing your dress

$ 0 for cleaning your bathroom

$ 0 for taking you to the Doctor

$ 0 for the present on your birthday

$ 0 for taking you to the school and bringing you back

Finally, dear son, you owe me nothing; because I love you.

The son read this note and was deeply touched.

Children are not against advice; but they are very sensitive to the way it is given. Remember, "The heart of education is the education of the heart."

"How can I learn to advise like this?" asks the mother."

Reflect on this:

Look at the way mother birds build nest. They build in such a way that when it rains, not a drop of water falls inside the nest. How does the bird learn to achieve such an engineering feat? It is said that, when a bird becomes pregnant, this knowledge arises intuitively within her. Love for her offspring brings out this latent wisdom.

Let your love and your fear guide you.

Your love will show you the way.

The mother nods in affirmation that love is the supreme power. She then asks, "How shall I deal with children's boredom despite the variety in entertainment through media?"

Reflect on this story:

A boy complained to his grandmother, "No one likes me at school. There is no joy in my life. My teachers reprimand me, my friends are better than me in sports, some friends are better than me in studies and I feel bitter about life."

"Shall I make a cake for you?", asked the grandmother.

"Good, I badly need something to sweeten my life", the boy replied.

After some time, she gave him some flour. "This is not cake, it is so bitter", screamed the boy. Then she gave him a pinch of baking powder.

Again the boy screamed, "This is not cake, it is so bitter"

Then she gave him an egg.

"This is not cake, it is not tasty", screamed the boy.

Then the grandmother lovingly told the boy, "Individually none of these things is tasty but when we mix them together, they turn into something sweet and tasty. In the same way, your experiences are bitter when taken one by one; but join them together with commitment and confidence. Add the sugar of your being. Feel them transform into a cake. Life is like cooking and you are the chef in-charge."

Reflections

Yoga of Wisdom

Power of Love is God.
Love for Power is Ego.

Yoga of Action

Love recognises opportunities and does not wait for its introduction.

Contemplation

Children are not against advice.

Life is like cooking, you should just make it.

It is an unhealthy bird that fouls its own nest.

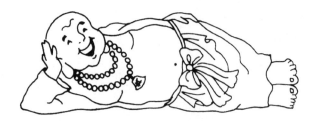

THE ANT AND ITS PHILOSOPHY

This is a real life story.

A person who met me said, "I was born in Bombay, and now I am settled in New York. I leave home at 7.30 a.m. for work and am back only at 8.30 p.m. I have to achieve my organizational goals and at the same time give quality time to my wife and family. I am tense and I don't know how to go about organizing my life... and I find that my life is imbalanced."

I said, "The fact is, you are busy and have chosen to live in a busy city. It is your choice. Now add a different dimension to your choice , and, in spite of being busy, you will learn to be relaxed, balanced and make your relationships work beautifully. Life is like painting, not like arithmetic. An artist creates his/her own world through a subjective vision."

The person asked, "What should I do, in the midst of my busy schedule, how can I give quality time to my wife and family? How can I be relaxed and reach my organizational goals as well?"

I said, "Look at an ant, and learn to organize your life. Ants overcome several life-threatening obstacles in this vast world."

"An ant?", he was incredulous.

If you observe an ant, you can learn a lot.

- When an ant encounters an obstacle, it is so flexible that it may decide to go *around* it, *under* it or *above* it. Flexibility is a great quality of an   ant.

- An ant never quits, but remains focused on its goal. It has the attitude of "Winners never quit; Quitters never win."

- When it is summer, it prepares for winter – Tremendous planning ability.

- When it is winter, it waits patiently for summer – Patience.

- At any given time, it does all that is possible; Totality of commitment

    However small it is, it never belittles its strengths – Trust in oneself.

- It operates in a TEAM –Together Empowering to Achieve More.

- Ants have the humility to follow the Leader- Humility is Strength, not Weakness.

- United, they build an ant hill - an engineering marvel in which even the air-conditioning effect is achieved - individual contribution to Team intelligence and Team Goals.

- Ants, while moving in a chain, exhibit perfect co-ordination in sending feedback to the ants following them about the path. This communication chain has perfect networking - Effective Communication.

"Organize and balance your life like an ant", I said. I elaborated further, saying we can ask these questions based on an ant's qualities:

- Flexibility: Are you flexible in allocating time to various activities? Can you appreciate your wife in a way that is life-enriching? Isn't flexibility the mother of creativity?

- Planning: In summer, i.e., when everything is going well, are you preparing for winter i.e., for the hard days ahead? Or are you lost in savoring the pleasures of the present?

- Patience: In winter, during difficult days, are you mature enough to be patient and have an understanding of the cyclicity of seasons?

- Ability to enjoy each moment: Can you consider every incident as joyous and totally rejoice in the present rather than desiring that one or some of your joyous moments be permanent?

- Commitment: Are you giving your best to you present endeavors? Are you allowing yourself to do better than your best and make it a habit to be fully involved in everything?

- TEAM: Can you drop the "I" in you and operate from a "WE - perspective" and make your family a team?

- Humility: Can you be humble enough to follow the rules of life rather than treating rules as conditions constraining your natural flow? Can discipline become a harnessing force?

- Networking ability: Can you network efficiently with people for accomplishing long-term goals?

Have you created an efficient ant hill?

Follow this philosophy, and let the results speak for themselves.

Oh, Mind Relax Please! Relaxation leads to balance and peace. Take your struggles as sacred, spiritual.

Reflections

Yoga of Wisdom

Life is like Painting and not Arithmetic.
Create your world of Joy.

Yoga of Action

Follow the Wisdom of the Ants.

Contemplation

What the human mind can conceive, believe and dare, it can surely accomplish.

Our struggles have a cosmic purpose.

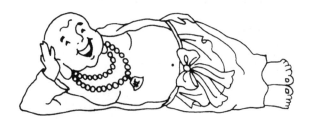

RELATIONSHIP –
A SACRED STRUGGLE

A lady, her eyes betraying an inner strain, but with a forced smile on her lips, asked me, "I feel miserable. My marriage did not work, I am divorced, my son constantly falls sick, and I am struggling to make ends meet. Do all these have some purpose, or is God playing with me for HIS fun? I become impatient and restless in my office. How shall I handle my impatience and my misery? I feel tense. Is there a way out?"

Moved by pity, I said, "If your marriage has failed, can you not treat failure as a learning experience? Failure is a fertilizer for success. Failure is God's or nature's way of teaching us something that is profound."

"How can I look at failure that way?" asked the lady.

I said, "Many times relationships do not work because men and women are not sensitive to each other's needs and feelings. This insensitivity leads one to ride rough shod and another."

Once this happens, one becomes unhappy, and considers the other responsible for it. Then each is busy counting one's hurts, and trying to settle scores with the other. Being aware of each other's sensitivities helps in understanding each other very well.

"There is so much of struggle in my life, why?", cried the lady.

I asked, "Are you a sportswoman?"

"Yes", she replied in a soft voice.

I asked her, "In sports don't we struggle to reach the top?"

"Yes", the lady answered.

Struggle is integral to life. Make your struggles sacred, give them eyes to see, ears to hear, a heart to feel, and legs to walk. Then you will have implanted sacredness in your struggle, which in turn will lead you up the ladder of success.

"This is going to take time", she said.

We should learn to wait with understanding and commitment.

Reflect on this story:

A man went to a shop, picked up a beautiful cup and said, "How nice! This cup is so beautiful."

Suddenly the cup started talking to the man. "Yes, friend, I am beautiful right now, but do you know what I was like before the potter fashioned me on his wheel?"

I was just mud when the potter scooped me out from mother earth. I writhed in pain when I was dug out. But the potter said, "Just wait." Then he kneaded me. I felt giddy when I was thrown on his wheel. I asked him "Why are you so cruel?" The potter said "Just wait." Then he put me into burning oven and baked me. I felt completely burnt. There was tremendous pain and I asked him again "Why are you so cruel?." He said, "Just wait." After that he dipped me in hot paint. I felt scalded. I again asked him "Why are you so cruel?" He replied, "Just wait." He put me into an oven again, I was in such agony that I pleaded with the potter to leave me free. He said, "Just wait." Finally he took me to a mirror and said "Now look at yourself". Lo, what a change! I found myself so beautiful."

We have to wait; our struggles have a cosmic purpose. it pains us to see things no going according to our agenda. But the universe has its own plans. We have to wait and make our struggles sacred.

Oh, Mind Relax Please!

Reflections

Yoga of Wisdom

Surrender to the Cosmic plan;
do not be a victim to your agenda.

Yoga of Action

Make your struggles sacred. Greatness lies not in
being strong but in the right use of sacred strength.

INTELLECT IS AN ANT; LIFE IS AN ELEPHANT

Some time back I was in Baroda to give a discourse on the Bhagavad Gita. There, a lady sought to meet me alone. As soon as we met, she began to weep uncontrollably. Since I felt that she would feel relieved if she poured out her heart, I encouraged her to talk. She said, "I don't think any one else in this world has suffered the way I have. I am going through such misery". She told her story.

Even when I was a little girl, my father used to molest me to satisfy his lust. Though I was utterly devastated inside, I did not know how to stop him. As I grew into womanhood, my father continued his incestuous behavior. I suffered this abuse every day. Later I got married. My husband was very loving. But my sufferings did not end. My father did not change his habit and continued to fulfill his sexual need through me. As I could not tolerate this any longer, I revealed everything to my husband in the hope that he would free me from this hell. But as a result of this, my husband also deserted me. Why? Why has this happened to me? She wept bitterly.

I could have replied to her question with the help of Hindu scriptures. I could have told her that it was the result of her sins in her previous birth! Or, I could have explained it on the basis of psychology saying, "Perhaps your mother may not have satisfied your father sufficiently. Or may be your father is suffering from some kind of mental abnormality and has not sought treatment for it."

If we could answer the question posed by that lady, then we could also explain to why people like Hitler and Mussolini are born. In fact, we could find a way to prevent such villainous persons from being born !

What can you learn from this example?

If we can compare our intellect to an ant, then we should take life in this world to be like an elephant.

An ant shouted to an elephant, "Come out, you big fellow, I have to talk to you urgently."

The elephant came out and asked, "Hey! Little fellow, why are you screaming? What business have you with me?"

The ant said, "I want to see if you are wearing my swimming trunks."

Isn't it ridiculous? Our intellect is like that ant. It cannot comprehend the mysteries of the world. For life is like an elephant."

But, just because we cannot comprehend or control complexities, it does not mean we should tolerate everything; and silently bear the insults heaped on us by others.

We should learn to be assertive, not aggressive. Assertive people never give up their rights. They do not allow others to encroach into their rights. We should face all the odds and fight them. But, whatever the result of all these struggles, we should have the mental maturity to accept them as part of the way of the world. Remember the crocodile's words "Such is the way of the world ; such is life"

Understand that life is not cruel, but mysterious. Mystery is to be felt rather than to be solved. On experiencing the mystery of life, we feel an intuitive ability emerging in us, like a mother bird's architectural expertise emerges when it has to build a nest for its offspring. Where does it originate? In the power of love.

I told this lady that against this background, it is not relevant to ask, "Why me?" Pain or suffering would be unable to hurt us .

Perhaps this prayer will help you.

"Oh God! Give me the strength to change what I ought to change,

Give me the courage to accept what I cannot change and

Give me the serenity to know the difference."

Reflections

Yoga of Wisdom

*Watch - Many things are beyond our comprehension.
Life is not a problem, but a mystery*

Yoga of Action

*Hug each moment of your life and
nourish your connection to the universe*

Contemplation

Gratitude for existence should be as regular as our heartbeats.

The greatest benediction is a true friend. So is good communication.

Among thorns grow roses. Among difficulties let love flower.

Hurt is hell's junkyard.

Hurt or upset whether justified or not justified is self damaging.

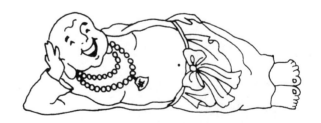

A CAT CHAINED TO A PILLAR!

What is prayer?

Here, we are entering the realm of God and spirituality. We need to think deeply. The essence of prayer is the ability to totally understand ourselves. A prayer is not a concatenation of sounds, words or sentences. It is mainly a sacred understanding of ourselves ; understanding enabled by devotion.

Prayer is not getting entangled in rituals with no inkling of what they mean.

Here, let me recount an incident. Recently I went to a house where I witnessed a peculiar kind of morning prayer. Even as the prayer progressed in the pooja room, a pressure cooker whistled and let out steam in the kitchen, and the sounds of an advertisement jingle floated in from the living room. Do we call this prayer?

Lighting the lamp, decorating doors with streamers of mango leaves and similar other practices are performed as mere rituals these days. Many of us perform them mechanically without understanding their meaning. For example, tolling a bell in a temple is meant to awaken one's self to the God within, not to awaken God in HIS abode. How many of us do it with this understanding? Such farcical rituals are common to all communities, races and religions.

There was once a Guru who had mastered the Vedas and Upanishads. One day, when he was teaching, he saw a cat moving around. Though it did not disturb the Guru, it distracted the attention of some of his disciples. So the Guru asked his disciples to catch the cat and tie it to a pillar. As the cat's visit to the classroom continued, it was regularly chained to the pillar before the Guru began his teaching.

After some years, the Guru passed away. One of his disciples became the new head of that ashram. The practice of tethering the cat to the pillar continued during his term. After a few months, the cat died. The next day, when the new Guru began his talk, he noticed that there was no cat tied to the pillar. He said, "Don't you know that a cat must be tied to the pillar before I begin my lectures? This is our tradition. Go at once and find a cat for this purpose!" The disciples promptly obeyed his orders. People blindly follow tradition and miss the spirit behind it.

This is not to say that we should not respect traditions established by our forefathers. I have no intention to instigate people against traditions. What I mean is just this – do all that you do with sacredness, with total involvement, with understanding, and with feelings.

Some people call themselves devotees of Lord Krishna. What was Krishna? He was the personification of joy, happiness and celebration. But you may have noticed that many who style themselves as his devotees go around with long faces. At some stage, in some cases, devotion becomes devoid of love and compassion. Devotion becomes a dogma.

As people lose touch with feelings and cling to mere incantation of words, the whole philosophy of prayer is lost. These days riots take place in the name of religion. Riots result from the inability to understand the essence of religion.

People come to me with complaints such as, "We cannot afford a separate prayer room. There is a noisy factory nearby, The kids are always crying, and the wife nagging. How can we pray properly in these circumstances?"

There is absolutely no need for peaceful external surroundings for one to pray or meditate. It is possible to pray in a market place and without mantras and shlokas provided one has peace within.

How is that?

There was an arid open space. Under a scorching sun, work for constructing a temple for Lord Krishna was progressing. Workers were carrying loads of bricks on their heads. A sage who happened to come along asked one of them, "What are you doing?" and the worker retorted, "Can't you see? I am carrying bricks."

The sage repeated the question to another. He said smilingly, "I am earning a living for my family."

The sage asked yet another and he replied in a tone of reverence, "I am performing a very sacred task. I am building a temple for my God."

As we can see, though the actions are the same, the attitudes behind them are different.

All of us may not be so lucky as to get the job of building a temple; but whatever task we perform, if we do that with total involvement like that of building a temple, that itself is the best prayer. God gives us what we need in measures greater than we need.

Reflections

Yoga of Wisdom

*Tradition blindly followed kills
the spirit of tradition.*

Yoga of Action

*Don't work for Worship;
Work can be Worship.*

Contemplation

The most unintelligent of all is a person who refuses to profit from his miseries.

You can't de-mystify the mystery of life.

People blindly follow tradition.

I do not dance because I am happy. I am happy because I dance.

Prayer is not to lighten your burden but to strengthen your back.

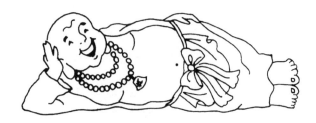

FOR SOME IT IS A HORRORSCOPE

Most often, our lives are wasted in fear!

In order to drive away darkness from his house, a foolish person was found carrying bucket loads of darkness and emptying them outside. Despite the many years he spent in this task, the darkness remained. His preoccupation with driving out darkness took him nowhere. Darkness is the absence of light. If only he had attempted to light a small lamp, darkness would have disappeared!

Fear is similar to darkness. Fear is the absence of love! Once the lamp of love is lit, fear will disappear. Let us take, the love between man and woman as an example. How does this love blossom?

Love is born out of the trust between a man and a woman. If they do not trust each other, there can be no love or affection between them.

Reflect on an incident in the life of Mullah Nasruddin, a character in Sufi literature.

Mullah Nasruddin got married just that morning. The same night, he and his wife were traveling in a boat across a river along with their relatives.

A storm broke out suddenly, and the river turned turbulent. The boat rocked wildly. Everyone in the boat, including the bride, was in mortal fear. But Mullah remained calm. The bride noticed this and asked him in surprise, "Aren't you afraid?" Mullah, without replying, took out the dagger from his waistband and raised it as though he was going to slit her throat. There was no reaction on her face. He asked, "Are you not afraid of the dagger?" She said, "The dagger may be dangerous, but the person holding it is my loving husband. So I am not afraid."

"Exactly!", exclaimed Mullah. "These waves may be dangerous, but Allah, who is in control of them, is full of love. So I am not afraid!"

Mullah Nasruddin had faith in Allah. So he was loving and compassionate. Without faith in God, he would have been devoid of love and compassion. Without love and compassion, even Mullah would have trembled with fright, just like the others in the boat.

We can apply this example to our lives too! If we are afraid, it only means that we do not trust our own existence!

We may have come across many who say, "I am God-fearing!" To talk of fearing God makes no sense. We should love God, not fear Him! The expression should be "God- loving", not "God- fearing!"

Swami Vivekananda said, "Be fearless. Fearlessness is the message of the Upanishads."

Some go from one astrologer to another with their horoscopes to find out when death would strike them. As far as they are concerned, their horoscopes are "horrorscopes." Such people are more afraid of the time of their death than its substance of their life! Such fear would devastate them both mentally and physically!

Talking about human fear of mortality, Rabindranath Tagore said, "Long before you were born into this world, God in his great provision had made sure that there was milk in both the breasts of your mother. How do you know He hasn't created another world for you after your death! So, have faith."

We can only advise all those who are afraid, to plan for their future; there is no harm in that. But any fear about the future will only ruin your happiness.

In order to protect your wealth, plan where to keep it safe; plan how to insure it against theft and so on! To live in fear, without taking any practical steps, is meaningless.

Instead of conjuring up images of disquieting possibilities like failure in the examination, use your time to prepare for and pass the examination! Life is a series of examinations; we need to pass them in flying colors. This is a tribute we can offer to God.

Reflections

Yoga of Wisdom

Faith does not crave for miracles.
But it often happens miraculously.

Yoga of Action

Faith does not move mountains.
But gives the power to climb one.

Contemplation

Very often a friend is not known till he is lost.

Help is just a prayer's length away.

Good understanding is better than silver or gold.

Let not the foolishness of logic prevail over the richness of love.

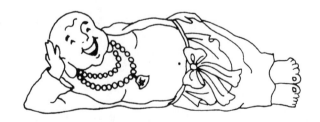

WHAT IS HAPPINESS? 1

One day, Mullah was very sad. A close friend asked him, "Why are you so sad?" In response, Mullah began to cry.

"My maternal uncle died last month. He has bequeathed all his property to me. I thought of that and am crying now!" said Mullah.

"I know your uncle very well", said the friend. "He was well over eighty, and his death is quite natural. Why are you so sad about that? In fact, you should be happy that you inherited his vast property!"

But Mullah was inconsolable. "You don't understand my grief, my friend!" he said. "Just last week, my paternal uncle died, leaving me property worth millions of dollars." He wept more, and was in hysterics.

His friend was really confused. "I know your paternal uncle too! He was eighty-five. Instead of feeling happy that you got so much money, why are you crying like an idiot?", he asked out of irritation.

"My sorrow is deeper than that. My grandfather, who was over one hundred years old, died yesterday, bequeathing property worth over 20 million dollars to me!", cried Mullah.

Now, his friend was really fed up. "I simply fail to understand why at all you should be crying", he said.

Mullah sniffled, wiped his tears and explained: "My maternal uncle, paternal uncle and grandfather, who were extremely rich, are all dead. Now I do not have any more uncles who will die leaving their wealth for me."

This tale signifies a very important truth. Greed is a prime source of unhappiness. If we allow it to grow, our joy and peace of mind will be the casualty. Happiness and satisfaction arise within us.

Water poured into a cracked pot will not remain in it. Similarly, people without contentment cannot be happy. They will only worry about what they do not have. Their hearts will always hanker for more possessions. Once the crack in the pot is sealed, it will hold water. Similarly, when the blemishes of the mind are removed, it will be filled with joy.

"Only if I get this and this alone, will I be happy", declares the greedy, obstinate mind. This greed gives rise to many desires. These desires in turn become blemishes.

For some, settling in USA is synonymous with happiness. For others, getting a visa to go to USA is happiness. It means, "Until I get my visa/settle down in USA, I have postponed being happy." Yes! Pinning their happiness on some event that may or may not happen sometime in the future, they let go of the present joys; exactly like a pot with a crack!

Such people cannot be really happy even if they do get a visa to go to USA. For, once they get the visa, they will postpone their happiness to the time that only when they get a job in USA. Even if they get a job in USA, will they be happy? No. The desire increases a little more. "Until I get a green card, there is no happiness!" Once that is achieved, they feel that there is no peace in American life; it is only available in India where all their relatives live! Thus, they would again postpone their happiness.

There are people who think that happiness is sold in shops. Yes, they resort to deriving happiness from cigarettes, alcohol, etc.

I am reminded of a story told by Ramana Maharishi .

A rich man had a pet dog and took care of it very well. But the dog did not enjoy the meals served to it. Like any other being, it too wanted a change. It left the house and wandered on the street looking out for food. It roamed around in vain for days together. It was unable to fight the street dogs. After going without food even from the garbage dump, it finally came across a dried bone. Being hungry, the dog bit the bone. The dry bone punctured its gum and blood started oozing out. The dog thought that the blood was coming out from the bone, and started chewing harder.

A wise dog looked at it and said, "Hey! The blood is coming from your gums and not from the bone; it is only a dried bone that you are chewing." The dog looked at it with disdain and said, "Until I bit the bone, my tongue had not known the taste of blood! Only after biting this bone, did I come to know this taste. So, the blood is coming from the bone. You cannot trick me!" Saying so, the dog bit the bone with greater gusto.

Similarly someone may say, "Before I came in contact with this object, I was not happy. After I came in contact with it, I am happy. Ergo, happiness comes from this object." This is canine logic!

Think for a while! Is there any difference between the dog biting the dried-bone and those human beings trying to find solace in cigarettes and alcohol?

Reflections

Yoga of Wisdom

We are Victims of our Limiting Logic

Yoga of Action

*Create the Energy of Rejoicing
in what you have rather than
Complaining about what
you do not have*

Contemplation

Where there is trust there is no fear.

I am an optimist. It does not seem too much use being anything else.

..Sir Winston Churchill

The highest knowledge is the knowledge of happiness.

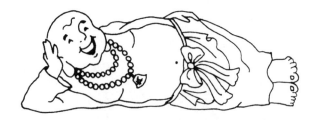

WHAT IS HAPPINESS? 2

A rich man went in search of happiness. He traveled to several countries. He was not happy. He chased wine, women and other addictions, but at heart he remained unhappy.

Someone told him that there was happiness in a life of renunciation. So, he decided to try that too. He packed all his wealth, the treasures stored in his house, diamonds, precious stones, gold, everything. He took the bundle and placed it at the feet of a Yogi and said, "Swamiji! I am placing all my wealth at your feet! I don't need them any more. I only seek peace of mind and happiness! Where is peace?" Saying thus, he fell at the feet of the Yogi in total surrender.

The Yogi did not seem to heed his words at all. He furtively opened the bundle and checked the contents. It was full of dazzling diamonds and glittering gold. In a flash, the Yogi tied up the bundle and started running with it.

The rich man was shocked. "Oh, no! I have surrendered my wealth to a cheat, a pseudo godman! What a blunder!", he thought. His sadness turned to anger and he ran behind the Yogi in hot pursuit.

The Yogi was unable to run fast. He went into all the lanes and by-lanes, but finally reached the place from where he had started his run. The rich man also reached the same place, panting hard. Before he could utter a word, the Yogi said, "Hey, did you get scared that I would abscond with your wealth? Here, take it! I have no need for it. You can keep it for yourself!" and returned the bundle to him.

The rich man was very happy that he got back his "lost" wealth. "Here is peace", said the Yogi. "You see, all this wealth was with you even before you came here. But you did not derive joy from them. It is the same wealth that is with you now, but now you have found great joy in your heart! Where did that happiness come from? From the wealth, or from within you?"

It is clear from the story that joy and happiness are not outside us. They are within us!

The Kingdom of heaven is within you, says the Bible.

Just like the rich man who went around with the bundle of wealth, many of us do not realize this truth. That is the reason why we look up to others for our happiness.

When the boss appreciates our work, "Good, you did a fine job!" we literally float in the air. When he utters a word of criticism, all happiness deserts us! So we become like a football to be kicked by others.

A drunkard lay unconscious in the street. A friend who happened to come by said to him jokingly, "Hey, I went to your house. I found that your wife has become a widow. So go home quickly and console her!"

The drunkard was very upset. "Oh, no! My wife has become a widow!" He began to cry. "How can your wife become a widow when you are alive?", asked a passer by. The drunkard answered, "But my friend told me that my wife has become a widow. He is my close friend and how can I disbelieve him?" The drunkard continued to cry. Our sorrow is similar to that of the drunkard. The sorrow he experienced was uncalled for as it was born out of ignorance.

In each of us, there is a drunkard. Many things strike us as unpalatable because of their superficial unpleasantness. On analysis, however, they prove harmless. At other times, matters which are not important manage to rob us of our happiness.

Here are some examples:

A young woman was playing with her child on the beach. Suddenly a huge wave dragged the child in. The woman began to wail," My baby! My baby is gone!" The God of the seas heard her cry, and returned the child alive to the shore. The woman was overjoyed and hugged her child and showered kisses on its cheeks. Glancing at its feet, she noticed that one of the sandals was missing. At once, her joy was shattered and she began to wail again for the missing footwear. This is how we miss appreciating the bigger gifts of life. We get lost in pettiness.

A farmer had a bumper crop of tomatoes in one season. Yet, he seemed dejected. His neighbors enquired of him the reason for his worry. He replied, "Normally, I feed my pigs with tomatoes." The neighbors enquired, "What is the problem? You have a bumper crop this time!". The farmer replied, "Yes. I have a bumper crop; but I do not have a single rotten tomato which I can feed to my pigs. What will I feed them with?"

To put it simply, happiness is like a lock and intelligence is like a key. If you turn the key of intelligence in the right direction, it will open the door to happiness. If you turn it in the opposite direction, the doors of happiness get locked!

Reflections

Yoga of Wisdom

*The Kingdom of Heaven is within you;
do not get lost in the trivial aspects of life.*

Yoga of Action

*For every minute you're upset,
you loose sixty seconds of joy.*

Contemplation

Unhappy mind often gives small things a big shadow.

Don't miss seeing the bigger gifts of life.

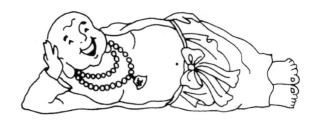

TENSION...TENSION...!

Certain incidents make us so tense that our blood vessels reach a bursting point! Most often, we get so flustered that our limbs begin to tremble! The heart beats loud enough to be audible to someone standing a few feet away. We experience a fear so strong and inexplicable that it makes us feel as though we were drowning in a dark sea. All this is due to tension.

Many a time, we get tense on trivialities. Here is an example.

A professor was transferred from his college. Four of his colleagues accompanied him to the railway station to see him off. There was still time for the train to depart. The professors, standing on the platform, began to chat. They were so engrossed in their conversation that they did not realize that the train had begun to move.

Suddenly flustered, they decided to jump into the train. Without even bothering about which compartment they were getting into, the four of them struggled with the crowd and somehow entered the compartment. Their idea was to move into the correct compartment in the next station.

But one professor, holding his luggage in his hands, was unable to board the train. A passer-by consoled him saying, "Don't worry Sir! In another ten minutes the next train will be here."

The professor replied, "I know there is another train in ten minutes. I am not worried about myself! I am only worried about my colleagues. They came only to see me off; in the process, they have all boarded the train by mistake!"

This is how tension and agitation make us lose track of even simple matters. When we are agitated, no matter how hard we work to accomplish some task, the net result will be zero.

Four persons went out to have a drink. All of them got totally drunk. While returning home, it was pitch dark and they had to cross a river. They looked out for the boatman, but he was not to be seen anywhere. The boat was tied to the mooring. They decided to row themselves home. So they got into the boat and began rowing. One hour passed, two hours and then general hours crept by... but they were yet to reach the other side of the bank. Soon it was dawn. Their intoxication was slowly receding. Only then did they notice that the boat was still tied to the mooring!

Just as the drink and darkness blinded the eyes of the drunkards, agitation blinds our minds on several occasions. We are prevented from seeing the truth and reality "as it is".

This is a story from Zen Buddhism..

A King wished to select a good Chief Minister for his Kingdom. In his court were four men equally qualified to hold the post. He therefore decided to conduct a test to select one from them.

One day, he called all four of them and said, "I have a lock. It is a scientific lock, made according to mathematical calculations. Tomorrow morning all of you would be given a chance to open this lock. The person who succeeds in opening this lock within the shortest time will become the Chief Minister of this Kingdom."

With a desire to become the Chief Minister, the men sat up the whole night, browsing ancient writings regarding locks, mathematical designing etc., and made notes. Only one amongst them looked at a few palm leaves and then went to bed.

The next day, in the king's court, the mathematical lock was brought and placed in front of the four men. The king was also present. The gigantic size of the lock astonished everyone. The four men checked their writings again and again. The men came up, one by one, and looked at the lock. They referred to their notes and tried to open the lock, but couldn't. The one who had gone to sleep early was the last one to come. He came close to the lock and inspected it thoroughly. He saw that the lever of the lock had not been engaged at all! So, without even using a key, he opened the lock by lifting the lever. The king appointed him the Chief Minister. The others, in their anxiety to open the lock, did not bother to check whether it had been locked in the first place.

To solve a problem, one must first understand the problem. To understand the problem, the mind should be calm, free of tension or agitation. This calmness will facilitate seeing things objectively, in the proper perspective.

How to be calm?

Just be spectators to your thoughts. Don't identify with them. See them as clouds in the sky of your awareness. Thoughts will come and go; but you stay. You are just an observer. Then the mystery of calmness happens. That leads to perception.

Reflections

Yoga of Wisdom

Life is like a Lock and
Understanding is like a Key.

Yoga of Action

Let Alertness be your Inner Guide;
not Tension.

Contemplation

Be alert and attentive to what a man is and not to what he has been.

If you are tense you are wrong. If you are joyful you are right.

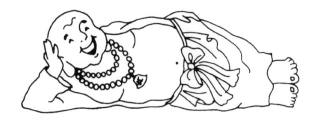

OH, IT IS THE SAME OLD GIRL!

Before we move on to answer your query as to how to reduce tension, should we not understand how tension is created?

Take a look at this scene -

He has to be in the office at 10 a.m. it is 8 a. m. by the time he wakes up after a good sleep. He has to be in the office within the next two hours. He hurries to the bathroom. The door is closed and his son is inside. "Are you dozing in there? Come out at once! I have to go to the office!" he screams, and when the son comes out, he goes into the bathroom. There is no toothpaste to be seen on the stand. His tension mounts. Somehow he completes his morning rituals and emerges from the bathroom. There is no time for breakfast. He grabs some clothes, wears them and is about to leave for the office. His wife calls out, "Please take the children with you and leave them in the school on your way!" He gnashes his teeth, but waits for the kids and drops them at school. On reaching the office, he slumps into his seat. His superior asks him for the files he had attended to the previous day, and his hands reach into his trouser pocket for the table key...uh,uh! He has forgotten the key at home! Now his body begins to tremble. So what is the use of his coming to the office in such a hurry?

Now let us see! "What is the reason for his tension? Laziness, lack of alertness, or lack of planning?

The next major reason for tension is a lack of fortitude.

God has provided us with eyes and ears. Despite that, very often we live like blind and deaf people. Above all this, we are arrogant enough to think that we know everything!

Even those who have all the material comforts of life have this shortcoming.

Here is an example - He is a great basketball champion. The college where he studied organizes a celebration in his honor. After the event, he expresses his desire to have a look at his old classroom and the hostel. The college authorities bring him to his old classroom.

Glancing at the room, he exclaims, "The same old room!" They take him to the hostel – "The same old hostel!" he quips. The smell of cigarettes lingers in the atmosphere... "The same old cigarette..." he says. Looking at him approaching his old room in the hostel, one of the college–students rushes to the room to warn his roommate, who is enjoying a tryst with a co-student. On being warned, this student hides his girlfriend in a cupboard. The champion, who enters the room with the college authorities, looks at the cupboard and says, "The same old cupboard!" The authorities open the cupboard and the girl jumps out. The champion says automatically, "The same old girl." The occupant of the room student screams, "No, not the same old girl! This is MY girlfriend!"

Just brush aside the comedy here and take a deeper look at the meaning behind the story. It shows that very often, we do not notice the obvious facts which glare at us! Our minds are hijacked by our past and are hence not available for an analysis of the present. Thus, the present is polluted by the past.

We can confidently state that we ourselves are the reason for the tension we experience. Circumstances are just that : merely circumstantial.

One individual cannot perform all the tasks. One has to delegate work to others. One would surely land up in tension if one were to say, "No one except me knows how to do these things. I have to do everything!"

Well then, how can we live without tension? What is to be done?

Tension is similar to noise. In order to make noise, one has to make some effort, like clapping one's hands. Freedom from tension is similar to silence. One cannot create silence. Silence is already there. Silence is the absence of any effort at making noise.

Similarly, effort is required to create tension. To create a situation *without* tension, your effort is not necessary; only a silent mind is necessary. Your thoughts are nothing but words. Words are noisy. Can your being be wordless? Then see the magic of silence happening in you. This is Meditation.

Reflect on this:

A farmer once went to a Sufi saint with a problem. He said, "My wife is rearing a lot of cattle and chicken. The whole house is stinking with their odor. I am unable even to breathe. You must show me a way out of this nuisance."

The Saint said, "Why don't you open the windows? The fresh air would drive out the odor!" The farmer exclaimed, "Oh, no! Then my pigeons would fly out of the house!"

Very often, we behave like the farmer when it comes to our tensions. In order to hold on to something insignificant like the pigeons, we refuse to open the window of wisdom. The result? Tension, suffocation. So, let us open wide the windows of wisdom.

Reflections

Yoga of Wisdom

Be aware of your unawareness.

Yoga of Action

*Create an energy of wordless presence;
be not a victim to a noisy mind.*

Contemplation

Knowledge is often a mask we wear to hide our ignorance.

Let us open wide the windows of wisdom.

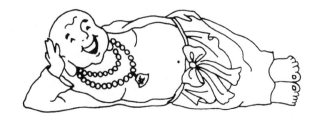

THE DAY THE SEAGULLS STAYED AWAY

How is life?

"Somehow it drags on!"

Many of us say "life drags on" with an expression of utter boredom. If we act with this attitude, we will not be able to move even an inch forward in our life. Our life would be bereft of interest or enthusiasm. Life without enthusiasm is just aging. How to get out of this quicksand called boredom?

Large corporations take good care of their executives. They especially try to ensure that they do not become alienated or apathetic. The companies give them pay rises and promotions to encourage and motivate them. They give them the power and opportunities to take decisions. Most important of all, they make them feel that they are indispensable to the organization.

Now consider this. Whether at home or at work, we become indifferent only when our sense of importance diminishes. If others get more attention, we feel jealous. It is this jealousy that leads to apathy and lethargy.

"Everyday, it is the same story! This manager is quite annoying!": at the office.

"This bus never arrives on time!": at the bus stop.

"If I see your face in the morning, everything goes wrong the whole day!" : at home.

It is not the bad manager or the buses that run late that make us feel depressed. The words and expressions that we use to describe the situations are the root cause of our depression. So, if you want to chase away the blues, throw out such words from your everyday vocabulary.

One way to drive away depression, and energize ourselves is to practice autosuggestion!

"Hey, Shankar! You have it in you, young chap! You can get this job done better than any one else." If we begin to talk to ourselves like this, fresh energy will begin to flow through our veins and our minds. If we become enthusiastic, the light waves that emanate from our bodies will make those around us also enthusiastic.

Does this confuse you? This is a scientifically proven fact!

When we say "I", there are three factors involved -

- the body

- the mind, and

- the waves or vibrations that emanate from the body.

When we speak of great leaders, we usually say that there is a brightness or aura around them. This aura is from the light waves that emerge from the body of a person.

There is a well-known Zen story. There was a sage who had realized the truth about himself and the world around him. Everyday he used to sit in front of the ocean and meditate. During those moments, seagulls would fly fearlessly around him and play. At times, these birds would even sit on his shoulders.

One day, as usual, the sage went to the seashore to meditate. A small boy who came to play on the seaside came up to him and said, "These birds play so freely near you. Won't you catch one and give it to me?"

The sage agreed, thinking that the boy wanted only one bird, and so it was not a big deal. The next day when he went to meditate on the seashore, all the seagulls flew well above his head; not one bird came anywhere near him! The birds were able to sense his intention from the waves that emanated from his body!

Your energy field will also touch people. Make sure you have good energy and create good vibrations around you.

One big industrialist I know was in the habit of giving his wife a signed blank check leaf before leaving for work. He had provided her with all the material comforts and almost limitless money. However, every time I visited their home, the wife used to complain, "He never comes home on time! He does not even ask the children about their studies."

As far as that lady was concerned, all that she wanted from her husband was for him to talk to her and the children for a half-an-hour at least once a week!

This is known as "value system" in management. The motivation level of a person designated as a sales representative" can be considerably enhanced by re-designation as "sales officer." This would be more effective than an increment of $ 200.

No matter how enthusiastic we are and how well we motivate our colleagues, even a small failure could hurl us into the abyss of depression. There is no denying this fact!

Do keep this in mind: Just as the experience of success is sweet, the experience of failure is also sweet. Success has its own flavor; failure has its own flavor too. We can understand this if we learn to view failure as nothing but postponed success! There is nothing in it to make us depressed. Treat failure as a fertilizer for success.

Treat each experience as unique. In this wordless experience, your being begins to relax. Then you will find that life is not a series of vacant spaces or emotional dungeons.

Reflections

Yoga of Wisdom

*Watch your Aura –
your Energy field, always*

Yoga of Action

*Love promises a safe landing though
not a calm voyage.*

Contemplation

Don't complain too much. The wheel that squeaks the loudest is the one that gets replaced often.

Your energy field will also touch people.

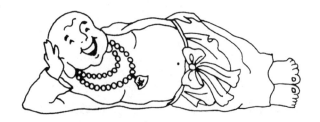

WATCH YOUR THINKING CLOSELY!

Depression, fear, anger, and disgust: where do they originate?

They do not rise from our hands, legs, lungs or respiratory canals. They are generated by our thoughts. Now, what is "thought"?

Consider this for a minute. When we allow words to swim silently within us, without escaping through our lips or tongue, thoughts take shape.

We cannot think without words and sentences. For the time being let us keep aside creative artists like musicians and painters who can think with sounds and colors.

A person starts a business. Along the way, he suffers a loss. At once he begins to think that he is unfit for business and unable to understand the nuances of running a business. These very thoughts within his mind would generate a complex of negative feelings. Let the same person, on the other hand, tells himself,

"Profit or loss is natural in business . I gain nothing by getting upset." These thoughts would enable him to face failure in a positive way and strengthen his foundation with lessons from his failure.

The following incident happened during the Second World War.

The Nazis conducted quite a few gruesome experiments on prisoners of war. In one such experiment, they told the prisoners, "We are going to kill you in a novel way! We want to see how you die when blood is slowly drained from your body."

As a trial, they put two prisoners in bed and began to drain their blood. The blood was allowed to drain into a nearby bottle making a dripping sound. After a few minutes, they tied their eyes with a black cloth. Then they stopped draining the blood from one of the prisoners' body. But the dripping noise continued to be made. The prisoner who was listening to the sound began to tremble in fear. He thought that all the blood was draining from his body, while in reality, it was not so.

"Oh, I am going to die in a short while.", he thought. By the end of the experiment, both the prisoners died.

In the case of the first prisoner, the very thought that his blood oozing out continuously was enough to kill him. His death was due to the impact of his thoughts on his body.

We need to understand a simple fact regarding the statements like the following that we usually make:

"It is so boring!"

"I am so tired!"

"I feel so ill!"

"Is this a child? It is a little devil."

Avoid using such readymade negative statements, not only in speech, but also in thinking.

Now what I have been explaining so extensively can be condensed into one word – "Language."

To start with, there is no need to control or curb our thoughts; good or bad. Let our thoughts run for a while, taking the natural course. What is important is to watch our thoughts very carefully; followed by the kind of words we use to express our thoughts. In a way, this is a basic quality required for meditation.

Let us consciously be on our guard against sustained negativity in thought and expressions. This will help us eliminate the readymade negative language that normally occurs in our thought and speech.

With continuous practice, stimulating and self-motivating thinking will become part of our natural cognitive and conversational style.

Let us make an attempt to be in full command of our thoughts, emotions and words.

What do we do when others make us angry by abusing and humiliating us? We shall soon see how to handle this question.

Reflections

Yoga of Wisdom

*Thoughts can make you;
thoughts can break you*

Yoga of Action

*No person is so poor that he
can not talk to himself positively.*

BEYOND POSITIVE THINKING!

Suppose someone expresses his/her anger towards us, or speaks to us in a belittling way. How shall we react to him/her? Listen to this story from the Buddha's life.

Once Buddha and his disciple Ananda went out as mendicants. When they approached a house for food, the lady of the house spoke to them harshly. "You lazy fellows, you are hale and hearty. Why don't you work for your food?", she yelled, and chased them away. Ananda was angry with the woman for her disrespect to his Guru.

"Please permit me to teach that woman a lesson she won't forget", he pleaded with Buddha. But Buddha walked away in silence.

A little later, Buddha handed over his water container to Ananda and went to rest.

After resting for a couple of hours, they resumed their journey. On the way, Buddha glanced at the water container and asked, "Whose is this?" "It is yours, Master!", said Ananda. Buddha took it, looked at it once, and returned it to Ananda saying, "No, I gifted it to you a little while ago; it is yours."

At night, Buddha pointed to the same water container and asked, "Whose is this?" Now Ananda said, "Master, it is mine!"

Hearing this, Buddha laughed and said, "I asked you the same question earlier this evening and you said it was mine. Now you are saying it is yours. How can the same container be yours and mine at the same time?"

Though Ananda was slightly confused, he replied calmly, "Master, you said that you had gifted this container to me, and so I accepted it. That's why I said that it was mine. Initially, when you gave it to me, I did not consider it as mine, because, even though you had handed over the container to me, it was still yours!"

Buddha smiled at Ananda and said, "Similarly, I did not take the words the lady spoke harshly as mine; so I did not accept them. Even though the words were directed at me, they still belong to the lady." That is why I said that there was no need to teach her a lesson."

These words contain a simple but profound truth.

When someone terms us as "lazy", we get affected by that word only if we take it to be "ours". If we are clear that we are not lazy, someone's labeling us does not make us so. The label is plain "nonsense", and nonsense should never affect us. In fact, we need not pay heed to anyone uttering nonsense!

If someone calls me lazy and I am deeply offended by it, it only shows my true nature as "lazy". A quality in me is pointed out by others. This is the root cause of feeling offended. This gives rise to worry and hypertension.

Now let us assume that a person is lazy indeed. Would it be possible for him to change? Of course, yes! Listen to this story.

There was a very successful businessman. He lived in plenty and prosperity. Unfortunately, once his ship got caught in a storm and sank. Soon after, his factory closed down because of labor trouble. His debts exceeded his assets, and he lost everything and became a pauper. However, during the next five years, he worked very hard and regained more than he had lost. He constructed a bigger factory, acquired two ships, and was richer than ever before! Learning about this turn of fortune, journalists came to interview him. They flooded him with questions about the secret of his success. His reply to them was, "I know that I failed in my business, but I never told myself that I am a failure. That is the reason behind my success!" Failing in one endeavor is one thing, and to treat oneself as a failure is totally different.

As we saw earlier, considering failure as a fertilizer to success – well, that is what our businessman hero did - is, of course, the best strategy.

You may feel lazy or lethargic and lose interest in work. But for heaven's sake, do not label yourself "lazy" or "good-for-nothing." If you do, you will become your own worst enemy, and prevent yourself from becoming successful.

Well then, in that case, what should one do?

Tell yourself, "I am not lazy". This is known as "Positive Thinking." But what I have to say here may be a little shocking to some of you. The truth is; "positive thinking" won't serve you in the long run.

Reflections

Yoga of Wisdom

More than the fact, it is the interpretation of the fact that hurts

Yoga of Action

The quality of your life is the quality of your communication to yourself.

Contemplation

Most of us are lazier in mind than in body.

The quality of your life is the quality of your self-talk.

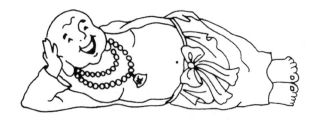

DO NOT CLOSE THE DOORS OF YOUR THINKING!

Whenever negative feelings like depression and low self-esteem raise their ugly heads, it will be good to boost oneself by telling, "I am born to be successful, I am a great achiever" and so on. This would produce temporary results, but in the long run, such positive thinking alone will not suffice.

Remember the advice to chant "Rama, Rama", every time a bad thought arises in our mind. Positive thinking is based on the same philosophy. Chanting the names of Gods certainly helps us overcome fears and temptations. But the temptations may arise repeatedly. Should one keep chanting *Rama nama* non-stop to control such thoughts?

Suppose, the whole house is stinking because of a rat lying dead and rotting somewhere. We do not have the time or patience to locate the dead rat and throw it out. So, we light incense sticks to stifle the stink. The incense may suppress the bad smell for sometime. But, once the incense burns out, the same rotten smell will pervade the atmosphere.

Positive thinking is similar to burning incense. Once its effects wear off, the miserable feelings will return.

Is there a better alternative to positive thinking? There is, and we shall call it "authentic thinking".

Let us assume that we are in deep trouble. We may lament, "Oh, God! My thoughts are always revolving around my troubles." On the contrary, if we turn to the philosophy of positive thinking, we may auto-suggest, "No, I am really happy!", and try to fill our mind with this thinking. This will only create a conflict within the mind, and not eliminate the root cause. Instead, look at your thinking from a distance; adopt a bird's eye view.

Without labeling your thoughts as "good" or "bad", without showing any aversion to your thoughts, take an impartial stand and observe your thoughts. This is seeing things from a distance as if through a bird's eyes.

Whether the thoughts are sad, bad or good, don't identify them with yourself. When you view them from a distance, a clear understanding will crystallize within you.

Once this mental state is attained, sadness and happiness will appear as two sides of the same coin. Happiness is an experience. Similarly, sadness is also experience albeit of a difference nature. For people who do not have peace of mind and clarity of perception, even happiness will appear as different from sorrow.

A father belonging to a middle class family had six daughters. They were all of marriageable age. Worrying about their marriage, he suffered a heart attack, and was admitted to a hospital. Coincidentally, his family received news of his winning a million dollars in a lottery. His wife worried as to how to break this good news to him in this situation. She requested the doctor's help.

The doctor decided to adopt a psychological approach. He asked him, "What would you do if you win $ 100,000 in a lottery?"

The patient replied that he would get his eldest daughter married. The doctor continued, "If you get $ 200,000?"

He said, "I shall get the second daughter also married!"

"All right! If you get $1,000,000?", the doctor persisted.

"Oh, come on doctor! Where do I have such luck? In case that happens, definitely I will give you $300,000!", promised the patient.

The doctor clutched his chest, and fell back dead!

If happiness is one kind of taste, sorrow is another. This attitude may be difficult to accept. When I was a little boy, I used to watch my mother eating bitter gourd with relish. I was often confused as to how she could really enjoy eating something so bitter. But once the taste buds take to it, even bitterness will be enjoyable. I later understood that just as sweetness, bitterness also can be relished. Every taste has its own uniqueness. It is not an accident that Indian cooking celebrates all the seven different tastes that figure in our culinary tradition.

Children feel that sweetness is the only good taste. They consider tastes such as bitterness, saltiness, and sourness as undesirable, and avoid them. We adopt this childish attitude towards life's experiences. We assume that only happiness is desirable and that all other feelings are to be eschewed; we close the doors of our thinking to most of our feelings.

Let us view thinking in its purest form. Let us authentically and objectively observe our thoughts and feelings, but not identify with them. Then the mind will automatically become calm. Truth will be revealed, and barriers broken. Life will blossom forth like a beautiful flower : softly, gently and silently!

Reflections

Yoga of Wisdom

*Don't be a Victim of an Experience;
but be a Victor.*

Yoga of Action

Experience the experience of what is.

Contemplation

An open mind understands an empty one.

One can always tell a failure by the way one critisizes success.

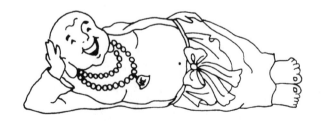

A CANDLE'S LIGHT THAT HID THE MOONLIGHT!

There was once an egotistic king. During one of his hunting trips to the forest, he came across a sage in meditation. The sage's eyes were closed. The king said to the sage, "I have fought many battles and annexed a lot of countries to my kingdom. My treasury overflows with the riches I have brought from various places. In my palace, there are many wonderful and pretty women from different regions, ready to please me. Yet I am not happy. When will I become happy?"

The sage, opening his eyes, shouted at him, "You will be happy only when I die!" He closed his eyes again and went back to meditation.

Enraged, the king drew his sword to kill him, saying, "I am a great king! How dare you insult me like that?" The sage opened his eyes again and said, "Hey you fool! I did not mean myself when I said I. I meant the ego. When the ego dies, you will be happy!"

If a person who has less education, status or wealth expresses an opinion contrary to our own, we do not accept it. It is our ego that does not permit us to accept it.

Consider this a little more deeply. An egoist expects others to accede to his/her point of view. "Every one should show respect to me!" That is the attitude and expectation. What does that mean? He/she would be happy only if others showed them respect. Simply put, they won't feel happy, unless others nod their heads in agreement with them. They are indirectly begging others to show them respect. When others do not give them the alms of "respect", they lose their happiness and their peace of mind!

Hindu scriptures talk of God as "Ananda", i.e., "joy." The word ego could be expanded thus - Edging God Out. Moving God or joy away from us is the state of ego.

In Hindu tradition, people break coconuts in front of God to symbolize the breaking of ego. While breaking the coconut, we indirectly signify to ourselves, "Oh, God! I am breaking my ego - "I", in front of you!"

Just as sweet water comes out of the broken coconut, even so does joy emerge when ego is surrendered.

Let us say that you happen to state your opinion among friends or in the work place. Your emphasis on the opinion is quite strong. Yet, somehow your idea is not accepted. If you were a person without ego, you would not worry much about it. Whether others praise your idea, or make fun of it, whether they accept it or reject it, you won't be affected.

Reflect on this incident from the life of Tagore. Once he was crossing the river Yamuna by boat. It was night. Under candlelight, Tagore tried to compose a poem. But somehow, poetry would not flow. Finally, he gave up and put out the candle. The moment the candle went out, moonlight filled the boat and the boat appeared beautiful! Tagore experienced a great sense of beauty. At once, poetry began to flow out of his heart effortlessly!

What is the connection here? The candlelight was capable of blocking the moonlight! In the same way, petty ego blocks the vast happiness our heart is capable of experiencing.

Reflections

Yoga of Wisdom

*Do not be trapped in the
tradition of ego; but purify it.*

Yoga of Action

*Attitude of ego-lessness creates
altitude of joy.*

HOW TO HANDLE A NAGGING SPOUSE?

I was in Madras to deliver a speech on labor relations. In that session, many top executives raised queries about unions and labor problems. After the session, the listeners left, except for one person in a dark suit. After ensuring that no one else was around, he began to speak to me.

"Swamiji! My work involves managing five thousand workers and five labor unions. Whether it is a canteen problem or bonus issue that leads to a dispute. I am the one who will have to settle the matter! So normally I am the first one to enter the office, and by the time I return home, it is generally late in the night. Due to this, I have to face a lot of resentment at home. My wife nags me saying, "Why did you get married if you could not attend to the needs of the family?" I can't take it any longer. If I spend a lot of time outside home, it also means I earn a good name and a lot of money. My wife too gains; she gets a comfortable life and high status. But she does not seem to understand any of this! I will bring her to you. Please give her some sound advice."

I told him of cases where women complain, "My husband is at home within half an hour after the office closes. Our children are all grown up. It is very embarrassing to see my husband hanging around me all the time, even at this age!"

No woman wants her husband to spend all the time with her from morning to night! All that a wife needs is "quality time" and not "quantity time." You are a busy executive. If you talk to your wife for ten minutes during meals, she should feel happy, but make those ten minutes exclusively hers! Open your eyes and look at her lovingly, intently ... not just dutifully. Remember how you used to look at her when you were newly married. With great eagerness and desire! Once she feels admired and appreciated, there is no chance for her to crib.

"It is not just admiring her looks. If you notice that she has changed her hair style, appreciate that! If the breakfast is good, compliment her saying, "Darling today you have done better than ever. Can I have another pancake please!" Of course don't make it sound routine or hollow praise. Make it authentic and real. Discover her good attributes and praise her whole-heartedly.

"Now, do not ask me, "Why should there be such flattery between husband and wife?", or "Where is the depth of such a relationship?" This is not flattery, this is genuine praise.

Even prayer to God is known as "Sthuti" in our land. Sthuti means praise. When God can be pleased with praise, why not your wife?

"The main reason for your wife's complaint is the inadequacy of your attention. She feels that you belong to her; she is not willing to give you up totally in return for the material returns from your official work. Each individual has to play multiple roles in life.

Finally I said, "Follow my advice. If that doesn't work, then begin to enjoy the nagging of your wife."

The ability to enjoy everything is a quality of an awakened consciousness. Your capacity for enjoyment should rise above your likes and dislikes.

The man left in what appeared to be total confusion. But when he returned a week later, he said, "Swamiji! Your words were wonderful! Following your advice, the two of us had a heart-to-heart talk after many, many years! Thank you!"

Vatsyayana in his *Kamasutra* speaks about the relationship between husband and wife. It may sound strange - but this is how he explains it.

The relationship between a husband and his wife begins in sex. The ultimate goal of a marriage should flower into compassion. I call this ladder of love as the incremental growth in relation between husband and wife.

Then it progresses through love, trust and devotion. Ultimately it reaches true compassion. I call this the ladder of matrimonial love.

Sex	➤	Love	➤	Friendliness	➤	Devotion	➤	Compassion
⌄		⌄		⌄		⌄		⌄
Lust	➤	Caring	➤	Non-domination	➤	Sacredness	➤	Forgiveness

Sex is linked to trust, love to caring, trust to non-exploitation, devotion to sacredness and compassion to forgiveness.

The relationship between a husband and his wife begins in lust. The next stage is caring - they feel for each other. The third stage is the friendship that blossoms between the two. In pure friendship, persons are equal. one does not feel that inferior to the other. They do not plot to ruin each other. There is no domination of one over the other.

When friendship develops between the husband and wife, both of them would cherish their relationship as something sacred; they would protect the relationship!

The final stage in this relationship is compassion. The basis of compassion is forgiveness. It is but natural for mistakes to happen. Forgiving another's mistakes is the last and highest stage of the relationship. Only at this level, does relationship become complete.

Can you transform your sexual relationship into a sacred relationship? In this process a spiritual intimacy will develop. If your relationship has a forgiving quality, then you don't bug each other, but lovingly hug each other. Only in this space is a relationship fulfilling.

Reflections

Yoga of Wisdom

*Distinguish between the usefulness of
Quality Time and Quantity Time.
Understand the ladder of Love.*

Yoga of Action

Learn to see Elegance in what is and Express it.

Contemplation

Ego is – "Edging God Out".

A shallow man is one who is full of oneself.

Transform sex into prayer.

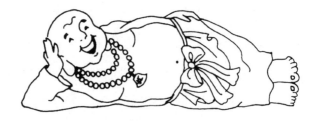

WITH FOLDED HANDS AND CLOSED EYES...

God has given us one mouth and two ears so that we speak less and listen more, but most of us consider our own voice the sweetest sound on earth! That is why many speak non-stop, with no sense of propriety.

In oriental philosophy, as well as in our ancestors' practical prescriptions, a great deal of importance was given to "listening". In order to listen to others, we must stop speaking. But, we do not; do we?

Inside the famous Sistine chapel, a lady was praying fervently, with closed eyes, and folded hands, to Mother Mary. Her lengthy prayer was nothing but a list of "wants." It dragged on like, "I want this...I want that..... The famous painter Michelangelo, who had been working on his painting close by, and was deeply engrossed in what he was doing, heard the voice of the lady pestering the Holy Mother. Just for fun, he hid behind a pillar and said, "My daughter, I am greatly moved by your devotion! I am Jesus Christ. What is it that you want?" The lady replied in irritation, "Jesus, please keep quiet! I am talking to your Mother, not to you. Don't disturb!" If a person is eager to speak, even divine intervention cannot deter that urge.

Some people talk endlessly merely to enjoy the pleasure of hearing themselves speak. Only when one stops talking, and starts listening to others will the importance of what others have to say be understood. Equally important is the interpretation of what one listens to is also important.

Buddha was talking to a gathering. He concluded his talk saying, "Do not forget to complete your duties before going to sleep." The disciples meditated before their sleep. A thief also heard Buddha's sermon. He asked himself, "What is my duty? I am a thief, and my duty is to rob. Buddha has endorsed my life style." Interpreting Buddha's words like this, he continued to rob everyday before he went to sleep.

Each one listens to one's own chattering mind, and interprets the words in ways most in agreement with their current concerns.

In the Holy Bible, there is a phrase "silly Christ." The word "silly" has a totally different meaning today. But during Biblical times, it meant "innocent." If we understand that ancient phrase in today's meaning, just think what pain it would cause to the people concerned!

Very often we do not listen to the ideas of others with an open mind. "Who is speaking? What is his/her purpose? Why does she/he talk on such matters in these circumstances?" Questions such as these ought to be raised and answered before we judge an act of communication. Many do not have the maturity to listen objectively. They are not willing to accept what others say.

It is only recently that western scholars began to lay emphasis on listening, but Hindu sages had made this point several thousand years ago!

The purpose of depicting Lord Ganesha with huge ears is to show that he listens carefully and attentively to the words of others. You may well ask for the evidence for this statement. The depiction of the body of Lord Ganesha as a whole denotes the concept of an ideal human being. The huge belly of the Lord has a specific meaning. One is faced with a lot of problems in worldly life. The God's stomach denotes that one should learn to stomach and digest all the problems of life and overcome them. The trunk of Lord Ganesha shows that one must develop multiple skills. This large limb is capable of picking up even a tiny needle from the ground. At the same time, it is also capable of uprooting a tall tree! The broken tusk of the Lord shows that one should master one's likes and dislikes. Our likes and dislikes are similar to ivory, very valuable. The broken tusk represents operating from commitment; not from likes and dislikes. The small axe in his hand suggests that human beings should cut away their desires and infatuations.

The mouse at the feet of Lord Ganesha is waiting for orders from the Master. Here the mouse is likened to "desires." The offerings – fruits and delicacies – induce temptation, but the mouse (desire) is only waiting for orders from the Master – the Lord. Desire should be one's servant; not master.

We can continue to expound on the figure of Ganesha and its underlying meanings.

Do make sure that all these concepts do not enter through one ear and go straight out the other! Let your intellect discern what is right and what is not. What I have tried to convey with the help of Michaelangelo, Lord Ganesha and Buddha has been put in a nutshell by a famous Tamil sage in just three clauses:

Whoever or whatever said it, it is wise to grasp the truth from it, no matter who said it. (Kural 423)

Reflections

Yoga of Wisdom

*God has given us two ears and
one mouth – listen more and talk less*

– Mark Twain

Yoga of Action

*You can win more friends with
your ears than with your mouth.*

Contemplation

There are two types of boring people

those who talk too much and
those who listen too little.

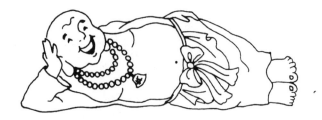

IT WAS THE FAULT OF RIVER GANGA!

I have the opportunity to travel far and wide, and to meet people from different cultures. Most visitors from abroad speak with a sense of wonder about India's rich spirituality, natural wealth, the unity maintained in spite of the cultural diversity and so on. They also ask me, why, despite such a rich heritage, our country has not attained material progress.

I have maintained discreet silence without answering the question. I ask myself the same question. My answer is that it is our "we-know-everything-attitude" that is responsible for our backwardness.

When we operate with an attitude of "I-know-everything", we fail to consider those issues unknown to us. The simple reason is, we cannot be open-minded as we operate with the "know-all attitude."

"Many of us remain blind and deaf despite having eyes and ears", Jesus said. That is why our country remains poor in spite of having rich resources. There is a story about this.

There was an excellent student. He learnt many things from his masters. Then he wanted to study the river Ganga. So he went about meeting scholars who knew a lot about the river. He spent many days gathering various details like where the river originates, where it is narrow, where it is wide, when it gets flooded, where it mingles with tributaries, etc.

After obtaining all these details, he prepared an elaborate map of the river and its course. He was quite sure that he knew everything that was to there be known about the river. Thinking so, he got into a boat at Rishikesh. He wanted to reach the Bay of Bengal, where the river merges with the ocean. The map matched with the fluvial flow exactly showing all the twists and turns at the right places. Now the student was intoxicated with his own knowledge and felt extremely proud that he knew everything about of the river. Suddenly, the river took a left turn. According to his map, it should have turned to the right. The student was shocked. But he was unable to accept that map could be wrong. He wanted the river to follow the map. He got angry with the river. He abandoned his journey and returned home. Since he acted on the assumption "I-know-everything", he was not able to fully experience and enjoy the mysteries of the river.

We create maps of people and want people to fit our representation of them. We adhere so much to our mental map of people that we miss the joy of being with real people.

Another bad habit of ours is our inability to correct our errors. Though we know that the mistake is ours, we justify our actions. The bigger joke is that we consider ourselves very clever as we are able to justify our mistakes effectively! A person noted for this mentality is called a "smart Alec" or a "smartie"!

A hawker was selling hand-held fans made of palm leaves. He sang the praises of his fan thus: "This fan is long lasting, it will last one hundred years. So the price is $5." The King, who saw this from his balcony, was amused. He called the man into the palace and said, "Hey, are you joking? How can this flimsy fan cost $5? It should not cost even one cent! On top of it, you say it will last 100 years. What a bluff?"

The Hawker said, "Your Majesty, this is a very rare fan. It can last one hundred years. That is why the price is so high!" The king refused to accept his explanation; but the hawker insisted on the quality and the price. The King agreed to buy one fan on condition that if it did not to last a hundred years, he would cut the hawker's head off!

Later, as expected, the fan tore within a few hours.

The king's men went looking for the hawker and brought him to the palace. The king ordered him to be killed. The hawker said, "Your Majesty! I am not afraid to die. But I really wonder how the fan that should have lasted one hundred years tore within such a short time in your hands! So, before killing me, would you be kind enough to show me how you used it?"

The King agreed to his last wish and showed him how he used the fan. At this, the hawker exclaimed with a hurt look, "Oh, no! This is where the whole mistake is! This fan would have surely lasted one hundred years, but this is not the way to use it. One should keep the fan in front and shake one's face from side to side, not the fan."

That hawker was a smart Alec, wasn't he ?

Reflections

Yoga of Wisdom

*One is an expert in rationalising
one's fallacies.*

Yoga of Action

*See what is, "as is"; what is not, "as is not". Then you
will find a priceless treasure.*

Contemplation

We create maps and want people to fit into our maps.

We are experts in justifying our follies.

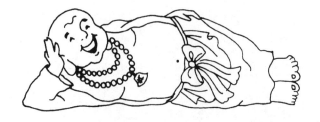

KAIZEN - CONTINUOUS IMPROVEMENT

Shall I talk to you about the principles followed by people of prosperous countries?

The people of the West have a certain attitude towards prosperity. Once they set their goal, say, production of two thousand apples per acre, they toil relentlessly to reach that goal. They would not worry about the fertility of the land or whether it is suitable for such produce. They would somehow manage to reach that production level, even if they had to use fertilizers. This approach is known as Result-Oriented Management.

The approach of the Japanese, however, is slightly different. They won't be very particular about per acre productivity of their apple orchard. Instead, they concentrate on the methodology of cultivating apples. "In what type of soil can apples be cultivated?

How often should the plants be watered?" Their whole attention would be on such matters. This approach is known as Process-Oriented Management.

The quantity of apples grown per acre by the Japanese may at times be less than that grown by the West. But Japanese apples would be tastier.

This approach of the Japanese is similar to the essence of Bhagavad Gita. "Do your duty without worrying about the results. For the result is interwoven with the very act."

The backbone of the Japanese success is the principle known as Kaizen. Kaizen means "continuous improvement." That is to say, no matter how well a job is done; the next time it should be done better.

Just as we greet each other with a "Namasthe!" or "Good Day", the Japanese say "victory to the river of life!" For the Japanese, victory is not a goal. They view each passing moment as a success. For them, life itself is a procession of victories.

When two people compete or fight, one person wins, and the other loses, isn't it so? Can both win?

They can! This is known as a "Win-Win" approach. Take the example of a company. Two executives are discussing a problem. One proposes his formula for a solution. The other's opinion is exactly the opposite. They are drawn into a heated argument.

In this argument, if one wins, the other should lose. But, let us assume that both of them view their proposals as solutions to the problem without bothering about who is right and who is wrong. Then they will reach a conclusion. The focus should be on letting both win; in such a space, a different energy emerges. This very process will make them happy and satisfied. In such a situation, both of them feel that he/she has won. This is Win-Win approach. This method is extensively used today by Indian corporates.

People generally operate from one of the following positions:

- I win, you lose   :   You are always in conflict with the other.

- You win, I lose   :   You start feeling low over a period of time.

- You lose, I lose   :   This is a sick attitude

- I win, you win   :   This is a healthy attitude

- No lose approach - If I win, I win; If I lose, I learn; therefore, I win (in other words, if I win, I rejoice at my winning and, if I lose, I learn from it. So one can always be a winner, if one has this attitude).

"I am keen to succeed. I have the necessary skills and capabilities. But my colleagues do not allow me to come up. They suppress me and prevent me from succeeding." Sounds familiar, this complaint, doesn't it? What I say may be difficult to digest. But please listen.

If a person is really keen to succeed, even if someone hinders him/her, she/he will succeed , the same way a buried seed breaks the earth's crust to sprout leaves. Even if it is held downwards, the flame of a burning torch is sure to rise towards the sky!

One does not seek the opinion of a tree to decide whether it is a good tree or bad one. A tree is known by the fruit it bears. Similarly, the world does not seek your opinion before deciding whether you are born to achieve great things in life.   Your potential for greatness must demonstrate itself by the fruits of your achievements.

Have an attitude of "I will better my best." Then an unknown power will arise in you. Interact with people with a "win-win" attitude and a "no-lose" approach. You will experience a mysterious power within.

Reflections

Yoga of Wisdom

While climbing the tree, grip the branches not the flowers.

Yoga of Action

Our goal should not be only success; but success and service.

Contemplation

*God creates opportunities
but expects us to search for them.*

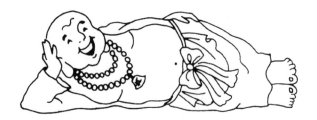

A PROBLEM OR AN OPPORTUNITY?

Problem!

This is one of the many negative words we use regularly in our conversation. "Problems in the workplace...problems at home... What a life?"

What is a problem?

Look at this incident. A young graduate was tired of hunting for a job. After many years, he got a job as a journalist. He went to the office full of expectations and apprehension. The chief editor called him and said, "Today is our Independence day. A navy vessel has docked in our harbor. Navy personnel are celebrating the Independence day on that vessel. Cover the celebration for our magazine."

First day, first assignment!

The young man ran excitedly towards the harbor. In the evening, the other reporters who went to various places like the fort, collectorate, party office and so on, gathered in the main office to give finishing touches to their respective reports. The new journalist was alone, sitting sullenly, without writing anything. One of his colleagues asked him, "Why aren't you writing your report?"

"It is all my luck! When I try to sell flour, a high wind blows, and when I go to sell salt, it rains! The very first day, my assignment has got me into trouble. The editor sent me to cover Independence Day celebrations on the Navy vessel. There were no celebrations on that vessel", the young journalist said dejectedly.

"Why?" the colleague persisted.

"There was a big hole in that vessel. People who had gathered there were busy preparing for the celebration. So no one noticed it. Only when a lot of water had entered the vessel did someone notice it. And then, they were busy plugging the hole and baling out the water. How on earth could they celebrate Independence day?", asked the new journalist. Hearing these words, his colleague exclaimed, "My God! That story must appear on the first page tomorrow!" and ran out to collect more information. The very situation that frustrated the new journalist because he viewed it as a "problem", was recognized as a golden opportunity by the other. The new journalist had missed an opportunity, which was spotted by another reporter.

Life does not follow a fixed agenda or sequence. It is a procession of unexpected opportunities! In fact, each problem is pregnant with possibilities.

Once Buddha was walking through a forest. The woodcutters working nearby ran to him and said, "Stop, please don't go forward! There is a veritable human monster in the forest. He is a cannibal. After eating the flesh of his victims, he cuts off their thumbs and makes a garland of them. He has so far collected 999 thumbs. He needs just one more to make it 1000. So, please do not go into the forest. If you go, you will only be courting danger. Why get in to a problem?"

Buddha replied, "I would get no better opportunity than this!", and walked towards the deep forest. As expected, the demon felled a huge branch of a Banyan tree, blocked the Buddha's path, and appeared in front of him in a cloud of dust. But Buddha did not run away like others. He stood strong, firm and said, "If killing me gives you pleasure, you may please do so! I agree that you are really strong. You have the strength to break a branch off a Banyan tree. But can you attach it back to that tree? It is very easy to destroy, but very difficult to create. You know the art of destroying, I know the art of joining!", Buddha replied. More than his words, the compassionate tone of Buddha touched the demon. After that, he became a disciple of Buddha. He was Anguli Mala, i.e., "the one decorated with a necklace of thumbs"

Let us not go into the analysis of the story. The moral of the tale is very simple. The danger from the demon was not a "problem" for Buddha; instead it was an opportunity to protect the villagers from further misery. That is all!

For some, even small matters appear to be giant problems. I met one such person recently at Madras.

Reflections

Yoga of Wisdom

Opportunity is "Now Here" or "No where"!

Yoga of Action

*Ability is the Alertness to cash in
on the Opportunity.*

Contemplation

You know the art of destroying,
I know the art of joining!

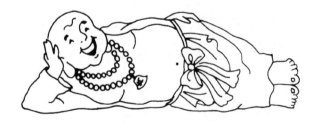

LIFE ENDED ON THE FIRST NIGHT!

There are many who look at a small thing through a magnifying glass and get terrified at what they see.

Recently I had been to Madras to conduct a training programme on self-development called LIFE (Living in Freedom, an Enquiry).

On the first day of the programme, a woman approached me and said, "My son refuses to listen to anything I say. If this continues, he may not even marry the girl I choose for him!"

"All right! Please bring your son tomorrow...I shall speak to him," I said sympathetically.

"Oh, no, Swamiji! Please advise him right now!" said the woman, placing her five-year-old son in front of me!

I was unable to control my laughter!

That little boy was refusing to eat what was served to him, and he was drawing pictures when asked to write the alphabet. Her question was how she could expect him to listen to her words when he grew up now that he was not obeying her even as a toddler. This far-sighted fear was her problem!

There are also other types of people, viz., those who magnify it out of proportion. They behave like a monkey that does not leave its minor bruise alone. It continues to scratch the bruise until it turns into a big wound; some even die of infection from such wounds.

A man and a woman were just married , and it was their first night together. The husband wanted to open his heart to his wife, somewhat like a confession. He began, "When I was young and in college, I used to drink with my friends. But from today onwards..." he was not even allowed to complete his sentence. The new bride opened the bedroom door and walked out.

"You have got me married to a drunkard. My life is ruined!", she screamed at her parents. The husband, who was watching this scene, was so filled with shame that he ran away, not just from the house, but from the town itself!

There is yet another type of people. They willingly put themselves into problematic situations. Here is one such example.

There was a well-to-do businessman from Pune. He was facing some financial difficulties due to losses. He volunteered to take me in his car after one of my programmes and I agreed. It was a sultry summer day. It was getting quite warm inside the car, so I started lowering the window glass. Immediately he stopped me. Unable to understand his behavior, I asked for the reason. He replied, "Swamiji! Many of my relatives live in this locality. If we lower the window glass, they will guess that I don't have air-conditioning in my car! Please bear with me until we cross this area." He didn't seem to realize that, in the process of preserving his false prestige, both of us were suffocating inside the car! Vanity prevailed over comfort!

We do face problems at times in our lives, true. At such times, there are two possible ways of escape. One is to catch the bull by the horns, that is, to directly confront the problem. The second is to go around the problem. If we don't overcome the problem, the problem will overcome us!

Well, how to overcome a problem?

Let us make a simple comparison here. Confronting a problem is similar to dating. Oh, don't get flustered that I am referring to "dating"; now, what is dating?

It is simply an opportunity for a young man or woman to find out about the tastes, likes and dislikes of a person of the opposite sex, isn't it?

View the problem like someone who is beautiful and is trying to "date." You will soon get to know the full dimensions of the problem, the ways and means to tackle it, and so on!

If you consider the problem as a punishment, you will definitely suffer. Instead, take it as a challenge, and you will feel energized!

Reflections

Yoga of Wisdom

We major on minor things

Yoga of Action

Learn to convert challenges into choices.
Failure in life is, who lives but
fails to love.

CAT... WHAT PRICE?

A lady said, "I had been married for long and was still childless. So, I vowed to tonsure my hair at Tirupati (the richest temple in India, situated in the State of Andhra Pradesh), if I was blessed with a baby." Later I became pregnant and gave birth to a baby. Just as I was planning to visit Tirupati, my sister's marriage was fixed. Now I was in a dilemma. How could I attend my sister's marriage with a tonsured head? So, in Tirupati, I offered a few strands of my hair instead of a full tonsure. Now I feel very guilty about the whole thing! Will this affect my baby in any way?"

In reply to her, I narrated a story. There was a very rich man. After visiting many countries for trade, he was returning home. While the ship was still at sea, there arose a storm. The wind was blowing at gale speed and giant waves rocked the ship. The man was terrified! He prayed in desperation.

"Oh, God! If I reach home safe, I shall sell my mansion and distribute the money among the poor!"

After a while, to everyone's astonishment, the storm abated and all was calm. The ship now sailed on smooth seas and reached the harbour safely.

Now the rich man regretted his hasty offer to God. "Why was I in such a stupid haste? Now, how can I escape from the vow I made to God?" he pondered.

Once back in his hometown, the rich man announced that he was going to sell his mansion. Most of the rich people thronged to buy it, competing with one another.

He addressed a large gathering and declared the price of his palace as just $ 1.

All those who gathered were stunned. "Has the voyage turned him mad?" they wondered. The rich man continued, "I will sell my house only to someone who is willing to buy my cat too." People thought it would still be a great deal. A palatial house for $1 and a cat to go with it!

"What is price of the cat?", a bidder asked.

"$ 1 million!"

The buyers were now totally bemused. However, as the house was worth more than a million dollars, one of bidders bought the cat for $ 1 million and the palace for $ 1.

The rich man declared "Lord! , as I promised, I donate $ 1 from the sale proceeds of my palace to the poor. Since the cat is mine, I keep $ 1 million. I have kept my promise."

We are so manipulative that we ourselves are not aware of our manipulation.

Does God ask us for this and that? We are the ones who offer all kinds of things to Him in the name of prayers and vows. We pester Him constantly, saying "I shall give you this if you give me that!" as if we were trading with him.

Some even stoop so low as to bargain with God, "If you help me get $ 2 million, I shall donate $ 20,000 to your temple", as though offering Him a commission.

One cannot call it a "prayer" when one gets entangled in vows and rituals without fully understanding their meaning. Prayer means fully understanding ourselves with sacredness.

The following words of Jesus Christ may provide us with some clarity at this point.

"I was hungry, you offered me food; I was thirsty, you offered me water; I was sick, you offered me help; I was in prison, you visited me; I was unclad, you gave me clothing. So, today I say unto you, whatever you do unto the least of these your brethren, you do that for me!"

Reflections

Yoga of Wisdom

Prayer is not a Demand Note.

Yoga of Action

The Divine honours no drafts where there are no deposits.
Let there be a deposits of
Gratitude in your Prayer.

THE POWER THAT MOVES US!

What is anger? When do you get angry?

Stop for two minutes, take a piece of paper and write your answer to these questions!

I used to ask the same question wherever I went to conduct the "LIFE" program. Here I give you some of the answers.

"I get angry when my children do not obey me.

I get angry when I am scolded in public.

I get angry when my colleagues make silly mistakes.

I get angry when people whisper behind my back"

The list is endless. Let us stop here and focus on anger and understand what it is.

When we think of ourselves as inferior, there is a reaction, which shows itself as anger.

When someone calls me a "donkey", I retaliate by calling him a "monkey." This is reaction.

When we react, external situations control us. In management lexicon, the word used with approval is "pro-active", not "reactive".

What is the difference between these two words?

The following Zen story throws light on this.

There was a Samurai. After winning a war, he was returning home with his army. On the way, he passed through a forest. In the forest, a monk was deep in meditation. The Samurai bowed and asked humbly, "Oh! Sage! Which is the way to heaven and which is the way to hell?"

The monk did not respond. The Samurai repeated his question a little louder. The monk still did not respond. The third time, the Samurai asked the question in such a thunderous voice that it shook the tree under which the monk was meditating. Now the monk opened his eyes and said sternly,

"You stupid fellow! Why did you disturb my meditation?"

Now the Samurai was really furious. He immediately pulled out his sword and raised it to kill the monk. The monk said with a smile, "This is the way to hell."

The Samurai realized his folly. The truth dawned on him and his anger abated. "The monk behaved the way he did, not to insult me, but to teach me the truth", he said to himself, and gently returned his sword into its scabbard. Now the monk's face beamed with a divine glow, and he said, "This is the way to heaven!"

When the monk slighted him in front of his soldiers, the Samurai was angry. "How could the monk treat me like that in front of my soldiers! I have been humiliated. How will my men respect me in the future?", he thought.

He was overcome by negative feelings, which clouded his judgment. So he drew out his sword; this is "reaction". To react violently and in haste – that is the highway to hell. To respond gently, and with understanding – that is the royal road to heaven.

"By calling the Samurai "stupid", the monk intended not to insult the Samurai,; but to instruct him indirectly but effectively through the Samurai's own "reaction". The Samurai was quick to grasp the teaching of the monk. Soon the sword found its place in the sheath - this is "proactiveness".

Heaven and Hell are but two states of the same mind.

When we get angry with others, we lose our balance, our blood pressure rises, and the whole body shakes. By being angry, irrespective of the situation around us, we suffer punishment in the form of anger. We and we alone are responsible for our state.

Reflections

Yoga of Wisdom

Reactive Mind is Hell;
Responsive Mind is Heaven

Yoga of Action

The Ability to Respond is Responsibility

THINK BEFORE YOU MARRY!

A magnanimous person visits a mental hospital. He distributes sweets among the inmates as part of his birthday celebration.

He sees a patient dangling from a ceiling fan and screaming, "Laila, Laila!"

On inquiry, he is told, "Well, it is nothing new! He was deeply in love with a girl. She left him and married someone else. That rejection made him mad!"

The visitor goes to another part of the hospital. He spots another patient in exactly the same position, and shouting the same name , Laila.

"Who is this?" asks the visitor. "He is the one who married that Laila!", answer the staff!

This is of course a joke, but it makes us look into the reasons why both love and marriage fail in many cases.

Let us look at ruined marriages in particular! There is a basic reason for this state. It is because we enter into marriage thinking that it would be pure joy! What a wrong assumption!

Lamp is not light. Buildings are not homes. Books are not knowledge. Medicines are not healing. Only when one lives with love in a house does it become a home. Only when books are read do they provide knowledge. Only by ingesting the medicine does one experience healing.

So is it with married life. Happiness does not come from the act of marrying a like-minded boy or girl and staying together forever.

If a husband and his wife go in different ways with different plans, their married life will not be successful. What is important is how they use each other's virtues for the success of their married life.

But many people who marry do so with the idea that marriage is identical with joy. When they fail to find the expected joy, they feel disappointed! Marriage is also like a lamp. Only when the husband and the wife light it together, will it bring illumination. Joy is exactly like that.

Recently, a young man said to me, "Swamiji, I love a girl and want to marry her. She is beautiful. She is also well educated. Her father is rich. If I marry her, I will be happy!"

He had brought his girl friend along. I asked him to bring her in.

"Why are you planning to marry him?:", I asked the girl.

"He is a cultured young man. He has a good sense of humor. He is hardworking, and is sure to come up in life. So, he can keep me happy", she replied.

Anyone looking at this couple superficially would immediately say that they are made for each other. But I had my doubts. If they got married with their respective attitudes, they might not be happy.

Here are a few thoughts that I shared with them.

The man begs happiness from his girl friend, while the girl expects happiness from her boyfriend. When they get married to each other, what would be the result? How can one beggar running after happiness, provide happiness to another beggar? Only beggary would increase.

My advice to married people is - do not think of how your partner makes you happy. Instead, think of how you can make your partner happy!

Marriage works when we are givers of happiness and not beggars of happiness.

Take the case of attractive objects. We are happy to receive them as gifts for ourselves. But isn't it much more joyous to offer gifts to others, that too, to one's beloved?

"Giving" opens up a higher center; hence joyous feelings arise.

Reflections

Yoga of Wisdom

If both beg for happiness, only beggary increases…. in a marriage

Yoga of Action

Marriage is a commitment to change each other's habits for better living.

THIRST...

The major trouble in married life arises when couples begin with a firm resolve not to have any difference of opinion whatsoever!

How could a husband and a wife born and brought up in different circumstances have the same opinion about a lot of things in family life, such as how to spend a holiday, what to buy with the bonus amount, etc.?

Sometimes there can be arguments between the husband and the wife. At such moments, one of them should be sensible enough not to let the situation degenerate into a quarrel. One of them should have a good sense of humor. But often, people indulge in misplaced humor. Look at the following exchange.

Husband: I got trapped in this marriage.

Wife: (in anger) You were after me; I was not after you. You used to follow me to the bus stop, office, home, everywhere!

Husband: (mockingly) Really, A mousetrap never runs after the mouse! It is the mouse that runs into the trap!

One can be sure that a flare-up would follow!

Another reason for spats between a husband and a wife is "comparison."

"My sister is five years younger to me! She has bought non-stick cookware, a vacuum cleaner! What have you bought for me?" There are many wives who complain like this.

Now the husband's response to this is also another lament "Look how sweet and cheerful your sister is with her husband! You are such a grumbler!"

Let me tell you a Zen Story.

A Zen Monk was surrounded by crowds from morning till night. Many would prostrate at his feet and worship him.

This became intolerable to the Commander of the local garrison. One day he went to the monk and asked, "I am the Samurai of this area. I have thousands of soldiers under my command. You are almost a beggar, looking to someone else for your next meal. But you get more respect and regard than I do! What is the reason? I feel bad and jealous."

The monk led him out of his hermitage. It was a full moon day. He pointed to the moon and asked, "What is that?" The Samurai said, "The moon."

The monk then pointed to the rose that was blooming in the garden and said, "Now, what is this?" The Samurai replied, "A rose."

Does this rose ever compare itself to the moon and say, "Oh, I am not white and bright like you"? Does the moon look at the rose and say, "Why am I not colorful like you?"

The rose has one kind of beauty, and the moon is pretty and in another way."

Even before the monk stopped speaking, the Samurai realized the truth. With moist eyes, he begged the monk's pardon and left in peace. Every one is unique in one's own way. Let us rejoice in our uniqueness.

There is yet another story to show how comparisons can upset some people.

A dog, having lost its way, enters into a forest. It is a scorching sunny day and the heat is intolerable. Not able to find water, the dog wanders all around. Surprisingly it finds a pond full of water. Tired and thirsty, the dog rushes towards the water. As it bends down to drink, it sees its reflection in the pool. Now, its thirst is forgotten and it barks furiously at its own reflection. It becomes very weak and feeble. Just then a wind blows, ruffling the surface of the water, and the reflection disappears in the ripples. Now the dog eagerly drinks the water, as it is able to see the water and not its own image reflected in the water.

Who prevented the dog from quenching its thirst? The dog.

We create our own obstacles by foolishly comparing ourselves to others.

Comparing ourselves with our neighbors in terms of possessions or acquisition blinds us to the wonderful things in our own lives, and around us.

Reflections

Yoga of Wisdom

Egotism is the stumbling block in the Head.
The bigger the Heart, smaller the Head

Yoga of Action

Mental dieting of Egoistic "I",
awakens the Divine "Eye"

Contemplation

Don't worry about the future. Between the bomb and the terrorist there may not be any future.

We are so manipulative that we ourselves are not aware of our manipulations.

Which is the way to heaven and which one to hell?

Today is the tomorrow that you worried about yesterday.

Marriage is the coffin of love.

Let us rejoice in our uniqueness.

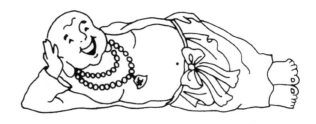

THIS MOMENT, THIS MINUTE, IS ABSOLUTE

Which is the most inalienable form of wealth we have?

I normally ask this question in my "LIFE Program."

Each answer is different. But I say, "This Minute, this Moment." No one can snatch it from us. But many do not experience "this moment, this immediate present" fully. This is a hard fact that we have to accept. Very often, we worry so much about the past or fret so much of the future that we fail to appreciate the uniqueness of the present.

At home, we worry about the workplace. While eating, our thoughts are not on the food in front of us. While bathing, we do not wonder about the fabulous body, a gift given by God! We do not feel happy that we are living today without a crisis!

Our thoughts behave like birds, flitting from branch to branch. Think of the result of such fickleness.

If our thoughts stray as we drive, we may meet with an accident. Similarly, accidents of various kinds happen in our lives because of aimless thinking. I am not saying that we should completely banish thoughts about the past. Nor am I saying that we should not plan for the future. I am only saying that we should savor each passing moment of our life the same way as we relish each drop of a cup of steaming hot coffee.

There may not be much difference between the first sip and the second sip. But, one moment in life is not the same as the next. Each moment is different.

In Zen Buddhism, there is a saying that one cannot bathe in the same river twice. That is to say, the water that is flowing in the river moves to another place, moment to moment. Similarly, life is in constant flux, each moment receding into the past. It is not enough to have education, knowledge and ability. One must also have an awareness of the uniqueness of the present moment. In the absence of that awareness, one's abilities and skills would be of no avail. This is the rationale behind the tests conducted by big companies to verify whether applicants have presence of mind.

There was an expert musician. If he played violin, it would even rain in the desert. Once he went to see a circus. During the performance, a bear danced to the tune played by the circus violinist. This musician approached him and said, "You can make only a trained bear dance to your tune. But my music can make any animal dance!"

The circus violinist rejected this claim as sheer nonsense. An argument ensued, resulting in a do – or – die trial.

The circus artist sent a lion in front of the musician. The lion, on hearing his music, broke into an ecstatic dance. Next, a cheetah was sent and that too began to dance. Then the circus artist sent a tiger. The musician continued to play nonchalantly. But the tiger was not enchanted by his music. It charged at the musician, thirsty for his blood. The audience scattered in terror. The musician threw his violin in the air and ran for his life. He somehow managed to escape from the tiger. The trainers soon caught the tiger and locked it up in a cage. The exhausted musician accepted his defeat. However, he was still puzzled by his failure to charm that particular tiger. The circus artist explained with a smile, "The reason is very simple. That tiger is congenitally deaf. In fact it doesn't have even ears. The audience found it out quickly. But you were so engrossed in your own music that you failed to notice this simple fact!"

All the wonderful skills the musician possessed came to naught because he had no presence of mind.

Reflections

Yoga of Wisdom

Be alive to the present and stay clear.

Yoga of Action

No one climbed a mountain just by gazing at it. Act from the present.

CALCULATING MISERY!

Male or female, young or old; each of us holds great power within.

The earth has its seasons like summer, fall, spring, and rain; the sun has none. Similarly, the body goes through changes of aging from child to youth, adulthood and old age while the mind is ageless. What is wonderful is that we can keep our *minds* alert and joyful at all ages and stages of our *physical* life!

"This is easier said than done", you may think. Is it really possible?

Yes, it is one hundred per cent possible. We need to practice certain things to achieve this. We need to see a lot, listen to a lot!

Every one has eyes and ears. Every one sees and listens! But is everyone full of vigor and joy? Think for a while! Every one has pens and pencils. But does everyone become a writer or an artist? Just as pen and pencil are mere tools, so are eyes and ears. Only if one knows how to wield a pen or pencil expertly can one become a writer or an artist. In the same way only if eyes and ears are used effectively can happiness be attained.

Most of us focus our attention on what is not in front of us. We don't see seeing things right in front of us.

A rich Italian father was celebrating his only son's birthday. The highlight of the day's program was a football match.

The stadium was swarming with people eager to watch the enthralling match between two famous teams of Italy. The crowd roared with joy as the teams competed with each other, but the birthday boy watched the game without enthusiasm. He looked at his father and asked, "Dad! Why are you so stingy?"

The father, who had spent millions of dollars for the celebration for his only son's birthday, was perplexed. He looked at his son in disbelief. What could he mean?

The son explained his dissatisfaction thus, "Can't you see those twenty two men out there playing with just one ball? Why weren't you generous enough to give one ball to each player?"

At times, we are just like this boy! We fail to appreciate the essential, energizing aspects of our life situations. Instead, we brood on meaningless issues and miss all the fun in life.

Recently, a young man visited me at my Ashram in Bangalore. He was complaining for hours, "My parents have done great injustice to me. My whole life is miserable."

When he was a small boy, his parents did not send him to an English medium school, so he was unable to speak English fluently. According to him, this single inability made him inferior to every one else!

After conversing with him for about an hour, I learnt certain facts about him. He had joined the same organization where his father had worked till retirement. He was appointed in the organization on the basis of its policy of providing jobs to the next of kin of retiring employees.

He had also invested a decent house in an extremely good locality. His parents had got him married to a girl of his choice. He had access to many good things in life because of his parents' benevolence. In spite of all these, he complained that this had been unfair. There are many such people in this world. Instead of enjoying what they have, they magnify what they do not have, and make their own lives miserable.

It is the habit of some to count pennies when they are on a holiday with their family. They don't cherish either the beautiful surroundings or the company of their dear ones. The joy of togetherness is spoiled by the arithmetic; thus converting joy into misery.

Reflections

Yoga of Wisdom

People are as happy as they decide to be.

Yoga of Action

Humanity's favourite sport is search for happiness. Search it wisely.

VISION THROUGH A KEY HOLE

This is a story about Mullah Nasruddin.

Mullah returns home from work and his wife finds a long, black hair on his coat. All hell breaks loose!

"You are having an affair with a young girl", she screams. Patiently he tries to explain, "Look, I walked through a crowded market place. Somehow this hair has clung to my coat. Believe me!"

She refuses to believe him, and continues to rave and rant. The next day, when Mullah returns home from work, she notices a grey hair on his coat.

"Alas! Yesterday it was a young girl, and today it is an old woman! You womanizer! Now my whole life is ruined!", she screams, rolling on the ground in tears.

The day after that, while returning home, Mullah remembered his wife's antics and carefully dusts his coat before entering the house. She hurriedly checks his clothes but finds no hair. Mullah is about to heave a sigh of relief, but no, it is not to be! His wife shouts in anger, "What a scoundrel! Today you had an affair with a bald woman?" and begins to wail more fiercely than on the previous days!

Such misery is the result of our refusal to see the beauty in front of us. We let our fevered imagination wonder and see things that do not even exist.

Even while listening, many of us fail to grasp important points. Or, we hear things wrongly. The result is nothing but tension.

Jack and James were close friends and colleagues. One day, Jack had a tiff with his wife on some money matter. In anger, he threw his wallet at his wife and left for the office. At the workplace too, he was tense. He picked quarrels with every one. His language was rude and insulting. James asked him out for lunch. Jack hesitated since he had no money, but James offered to pay for the food. Jack had not eaten since morning; he ordered a lot of food and began to eat. At the same time, he felt uncomfortable eating at his friend's cost.

At this juncture, James, with an intention to advise Jack on his rude behavior at the office, said, "Jack, you have to control your tongue!" Jack misunderstood his advice and became angry. He thought that James was referring to his eating by using James's money. Oblivious that they were at the restaurant, he grabbed James by his shirt and snarled,

"How can you behave in such a mean manner?" Now it was James's turn to lose his temper. Soon a fistfight ensued. In the process, crockery was broken. Jack fell on the splinters and injured himself. The restaurant staff intervened and stopped the fight. Jack was taken to a hospital for treatment and James returned to the office.

However, James was unable to concentrate on his work. He was full of remorse for his bad behavior and chided himself for momentarily losing patience at the restaurant. So he immediately visited the hospital to see Jack.

When Jack saw James entering the hospital, his blood began to boil, as he was still seething in anger. He concluded that James had come to continue the fight which had been interrupted at the restaurant. He was unable to see his friend's good intention. James asked out of compassion, "How do you feel now?" Taking this to be the height of sarcasm, Jack flared up once again and raised his hand against James.

More than the words, we need to understand the context in which they are spoken. This is the truth that can be gathered from the above narrative.

Unable to understand such simple matters, many amongst us heap trouble on ourselves.

Seeing and hearing, these two activities are performed not by our eyes and ears alone. At times, we view the world through our perception. The preconceived notions we form of persons and things in turn guide our perceptions. Through this keyhole called perception, we view the vast world around us. Most of these perceptions are foggy and baseless. Hence, our eyes and ears focus on the unreal.

Reflect on these examples:

Doctor   : Old age is the cause of your pain
Patient : Don't think I am stupid. The other hand is just as old.

* * *

Albert : How much did you sell your car for?
Joseph : "$ 20000"
Albert : "You got a good price!"
Joseph : "Yes, but, if I knew that rascal was not going to pay me, I would have charged him thrice as much."

Reflections

Yoga of Wisdom

Perceiver pollutes the perception and one perceives the perceived as an extension of the perceiver.

Yoga of Action

Renounce the distorted perceiver and rejoice the perceived

Contemplation

Treat problems as challenges and have fun with life.

Some complain that the stepping stone to success hurt and injure their feet.

Many people have faith in their doubts and doubt their faith.

An enlightened man is never confused by what he can't understand, but a fool is sure to be.

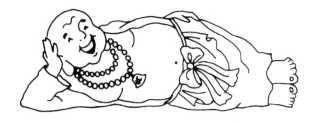

WHO IS THE CULPRIT?

The ability to see is a great gift. But we do not always see with our eyes fully open. Some of us use our eyes for sleep more often than for sight. Some others just float in a dreamland with their eyes wide open, but without seeing the objects in front of them!

We are awake. We are neither sleeping nor dreaming : yet, can we be sure that we are able to see things as they really are?

Many are not able even to look at things objectively. We normally wear glasses that color the way we see the world. By "colored glasses" I refer to preconceptions. Preconceptions are the opinions we form without any factual or rational basis about our relatives, friends, neighbors, acquaintances, and things.

Management workshops use certain puzzles to sensitize people to their preconceptions. Let me give you a simple example of one of them.

According to Roman numerals, the number nine is written as IX. Now the challenge is to change it to 6, by using a single line.

Now, before reading on, pause for two minutes and attempt doing it. Using a single line, change nine into 6. Why don't you try?

Here is the answer - Roman "IX", is 9 in Arabic numerals. Now think of the Roman numeral digits as letters of English alphabet. Can you see the letters "I" and "X"? Now simply add the letter "S" before them. Aha! Now "IX" has become "SIX"!

When I said a *single line*, normally the "mindset" in most of us would only allow us to think of a *straight line*. Why? The letter "S" is actually a single line, a curved line! But not many of us think so. It is only our preconception that prevents us from *seeing* the solution. That is, our preconceptions prevent us from seeing the truth.

Listen to this story...

It was a dense forest, full of wild beasts. A woodcutter lived in the forest with his beautiful wife. The woodcutter used to drink liquor and beat his wife. This agony continued for several days. The wife was soon fed up with the routine. She used to load logs into a boat, take it across the river, sell it and use the money for buying provisions. This was her daily routine. As time went by, she became friendly with the owner of the provision shop across the river. On a New Moon day, it was pitch dark. The woodcutter was drunk to his teeth and began to torture her cruelly. Thoroughly tired of his behavior, she came out of the hut in the middle of the dark night. A thought flashed in her mind, "why not go to the provision shop owner?" That would definitely be better than this misery!

Now she needed the boat to cross over to the other side of the river. She woke up the boatman; but he refused to ferry her across the river. She remembered there was a small wooden bridge across the river, about two miles away. She also remembered that a cheetah used to be usually seen around the bridge, but she was in no mood to pay any heed to that thought. All that she wanted was to get away. So she walked towards the wooden bridge. The next morning, her mutilated body was found near the bridge. The cheetah had attacked her during the night.

Now, read out this story to your family members. In the end, ask them individually, "Who was responsible for the death of the woodcutter's wife?"

One would say, "It was the woodcutter, the cursed drunkard."

Another would blame the woman saying that she was immoral and so she got her what she deserved.

Yet another would say, "It is the boatman who was merciless and allowed her to walk alone, so he is at fault."

Someone may even venture to say that it was the provision shop owner who enticed her into adultery.

The question is one and the same, yet there are so many responses. Why? It comes from the perception of each individual. Each one has his or her own perception.

In the night, as you look up at a peepul tree, you may only see its branches and leaves. Only when you peer through them will you notice the brightness of the moon hidden behind them. In the same way, at first, when you look at something or someone, your perception would cover your view and hide the truth.

Don't form judgments based on first impressions, stop; look again without personal likes and dislikes; look with a clear and unbiased mind at the same thing, taking time to assimilate facts, and you will then see the reality, the truth.

Reflections

Yoga of Wisdom

Don't be a Victim of your point of view

Yoga of Action

*Understand that there are many variables; Reward yourself
for the right action
that flows.*

Contemplation

Each one has his or her own perception.

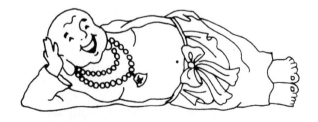

GOD IS IN OUR HEARTS - WHY?

One fine day, God wished to enjoy His creation and descended on the earth.

The devotees who recognized Him clamored around Him like beggars and pestered Him for favors. "Please give me lots of jewels! Please give me plenty of money" They chased Him with requests.

God ran from place to place in order to escape this nuisance. He went to villages, towns, and cities, but nowhere could He escape from the nagging. He found their pleas unbearable. So, He ran towards a temple; there too beggars stood in a line, with bowls in their hands. He was utterly perplexed as to what to do. Finally, He said to Himself,

"Human beings neither seek me within themselves, nor introspect. No one delves into one's own heart, so, that is the best refuge from this maddening crowd. No one will be able to see me." With that thought God entered into the heart of mankind and hid Himself there.

This is a farcical reply to a very serious question as to why God resides within our hearts!

Most of us constantly think about what we can get from others. So, we rarely pay attention to what we can give to others. Sometimes, if we donate a light bulb to a temple, we would like our name to be painted on it, even at the cost of the bulb's brightness.

According to Hindu dharma, when something is donated, it is taken as no longer belonging to the donor. In Sanskrit, *"na mama"* means, "Not mine." It is a mockery to donate something, i.e., to declare, that it is not one's, and then to have one's name imprinted on it as the donor.

Reflect on this awhile. Every thing we use in the course of a day, from the toothpaste in the morning to the mouth wash before the bed, is produced and made available to us by hundreds of other people. It is enough if I ask myself what I have done in return for what I have received from the society in which I live. Do we realize how deeply we are indebted to the world around us?

God has given us a wonderful life. Not all the brilliant scientists with their combined efforts can create a body as magnificent as ours. From the food that we consume daily, to this globe that rotates relentlessly, the wonders within and without, the gifts provided to us, are unlimited. How do we express our gratitude for this divine benevolence?

The very first teaching in the Vedas is to learn to be grateful. The Sanskrit word *"stuti"* means "praise unto HIM", and one must utter this word in total gratitude.

If we recount the words that we use frequently in our daily conversation, we will find that "Thanks" is one of those. We have to ask, "Does this really come from our heart or from our lips?"

A technical snag was noticed on a plane in mid-air. The plane began to wobble and the airhostess announced, "There is a small problem with the engine. The pilot is attending to it and soon it will be set right." But as time went on, it was obvious that the problem had aggravated and the plane was flying haphazardly. The airhostess announced, "Dear passengers! Inspite of the best efforts of the pilot, we are unable to rectify the problem. We are sorry; the plane may explode any time now. We thank you for flying with us!" Leaving the passengers to fend for themselves, she fixed her parachute and jumped off the plane!

So is our "Thanks" many a time, a mere formality like the words of the airhostess!

Reflections

Yoga of Wisdom

Existence gives us the necessary ingredients for our daily bread, but expects us to do the baking.

Yoga of Action

To know and not act on what you know is equal to not knowing.

WHY DO YOU SAY "THANK YOU"?

How to express genuine gratitude?

The word "thanks" should not be uttered mechanically. It is an expression of gratitude felt by one heart towards another. When someone expresses gratitude from the depth of his/her heart, their hands would join in obeisance, lips would tremble and eyes would well up with tears!

This is a story from Zen Buddhism.

He owned a small restaurant. From morning till night, he would toil in his restaurant. Yet, his heart was centered on spiritual thoughts. His only wish was to meet at least one Zen monk in his lifetime, but his workload did not permit him to go in search of a monk. Every one, including his staff and his regular customers, knew of his desire.

It was not the practice of Zen monks to wear saffron robes or any special attire meant for those who had renounced worldly life. They dressed like ordinary Japanese. So it was very difficult to identify a monk by external appearance.

One particular day, the restaurant owner was very busy. It was, however, his habit to observe all his customers. He noticed two men who were drinking tea seated at a corner table. As he watched them, his joy knew no bounds!

"Zen monks! I have waited all these years to see one, and now two of them have come to my restaurant!" he exclaimed happily.

The two men were Zen monks indeed. Seeing his excitement, they accepted him as their disciple. He gave his son the charge of the restaurant and was about to follow the monks. One of his customers asked him, "How did you find out that these two were Zen monks?"

"I found out from the way they were seated, the way they held the tea cups in reverence, the way they sipped the tea with gratitude. Every movement, every gesture they made, was filled with love. They radiated serenity", he replied.

He himself later became a Zen monk. He also established a novel method of meditation known as "Zen Tea Meditation" in honor of those two monks who led him to his enlightenment.

What is this "Zen Tea Meditation"?

Yes, you guessed it right! It is nothing but drinking a cup of tea with a great sense of prayer and gratitude. Even today, in

Japan, "Zen Tea Ceremony" takes place. In this ceremony, the Japanese hold the cup in both their hands, and sip the tea with deep relish, love and gratitude.

God has showered the Japanese with many blessings because of their deep sense of gratitude. But many of us may ask, "What has HE given us except poverty and hunger? Why should WE be grateful to God?"

In Islam, there is a sect known as Sufi. A Sufi monk and his disciples were walking through a forest. It was hot and humid. Thorns bruised their bare feet. Unmindful of these sufferings, the monk walked on and on. There were no houses where they could beg for food, nor any streams to quench thirst. Soon it was night. The monk and his disciples got ready to sleep, without having anything to eat or drink.

The monk prayed aloud, "Thank you Lord for everything you gave us today."

This really irked his disciples, who were weak with hunger and thirst. Controlling their anger, they said, "God did not give us anything today. Yet you are thanking Him. So what is the meaning of your prayer?"

The Sufi monk replied with a smile, "Who told you that God did not give us anything? Just as a mother knows what to give and what not to give to her child, God knows well what to give and what not to give us. Today, He has given us hunger, and an opportunity to fast. Whatever He does, He is right. That is why I thanked Him."

Reflections

Yoga of Wisdom

Discover the power of gratitude and existence will comfort you.

Yoga of Action

Value the power of gratitude. Let it be your mantra or inner song. Then you will grow and not just swell.

EXPERIENCE OF TWO KINDS!

This happened during US engagement in Vietnam.

The war had devastated Vietnam. People lost their homes, children their parents, and wives their husbands. The country was drowning in blood and tears and grief.

The American government deputed two commanders to Vietnam to assess the outcome of the long and costly war.

The terrifying scenes in the wake of war -- wounded soldiers fighting for their lives, mothers grieving by the graves of their babies -- so unnerved one of the commanders that he committed suicide.

The other commander also witnessed the same scenes. These, however, had a different effect on him. Troubles back home seemed too minor to worry about. After returning to his country, he spoke to his countrymen about the problems faced by the Vietnamese. Americans were concerned with trifles such as "The money that I lent has not been returned, so I cannot buy my next car." Many of them were touched by this Commander's reports. Soon, he was invited all over the country to talk about his experiences! He became rich and popular by narrating his Vietnam experience!

Now, one commander commits suicide while the other overcomes his own fears and helps others to come to terms with reality. The crux of the matter is this: both of them saw the same scenario, but their perceptions of it were different.

Let me give you another example.

There was a multi-national company making shoes. In order to assess the level of demand for their shoes, the Director of the company sent a manager to a country in Africa. The manager ended his tour quickly and reported "We cannot sell any shoes in that country." When asked for an explanation, he said, "People walk bare footed; No one wears shoes there. There is no potential market."

The Director was not a man to accept "No" for an answer. So he sent another man to study the situation. On his return, jumping with joy, he declared, "There is a huge market for our shoes in that country" "How is that?" asked the Director.

"People walk bare footed; no one wears shoes in the whole country! The market is huge and untapped", he replied.

This is what we have to learn from the story. Every person's experience is different in situations like work, trade, and home. But as far I can see, all experiences can be categorized into two types – good and bad. Whatever the experience, if a lesson can be learnt from it, it is a good one! If one cannot learn or has not learnt a lesson from it, it is a bad one!

> Thomas Alva Edison, who invented the electric bulb, did not succeed in his first attempt. He invented it only after almost a thousand failures. Someone once asked him, "You made one thousand experiments. You didn't get anything out of 999 of them, did you?" Thomas Alva Edison replied," How can you say I did not get anything out of those 999 experiments? Before inventing one working bulb, I learned how not to make 999 non-working ones!"

In every situation, see a possibility, like the manager who saw the possibility for selling shoes in a place where walked barefooted.

Reflections

Yoga of Wisdom

Failure is a fertilizer for success.

Yoga of Action

Learn from failure. Failure in life is one who lives and fails to learn.

NIAGARA SYNDROME!

Wherever I am on tour during exam time, whether in Bombay, Bangalore, or Hyderabad, students tell me, "Swamiji, I am unable to concentrate on my studies. Friends distract my attention from studies to topics like cricket, movies, etc. How can I solve this problem?"

Recently in Madras, I met a student who asked me the same question.

"What are you studying?", I asked.

"Chartered Accountancy", he said.

"That means, you must have been under one auditor for about three years in training?"

"Yes! Now my training period is over. I have taken up accounting work in a firm. Evenings are spent with friends and watching

TV. Even if I consider studying during nights, I feel like reading sports magazines to overcome my fatigue. As a result, I am not able to study for my exams."

Look at his value system! He gives great importance to his job during the day, sitting in an air-conditioned room with top executives! He values the earnings received at work.

Next in his value system is spending time with friends, watching TV and cricket matches. No one can say "this is right" or "that is wrong." If he thought passing in the exam was more important, then he would spend more time studying than talking to his friends. I told him this, but he did not accept it.

"Not that I don't attach importance to studies. Getting a CA degree is really important to me. TV is not important to me. But once I see the programmes, I am drawn to the TV and I immediately forget my studies," he said.

"It is because you give importance to TV that you have such interest in it. It is your thoughts alone that decide your actions. If CA is important, you must rethink your value system; you must try to change it", I said.

After two days, he came again.

"Swamiji! I tried to change my value system. But it is not that easy!" he said.

I asked him to write down the pros and cons of his choice among TV, friends, and qualifying in the exam. Grappling with the implications of each choice will help us clarify issues for ourselves.

The possibility of changing his value system by writing down the pros and cons brightened his eyes. I could see fresh hope dawning on him.

You have to plan today for your future happiness! Otherwise, sorrow and misery will encompass your tomorrows.

If you are going to rationalize that you cannot really plan your life and that the best policy is to take life as it comes, you too will become like the protagonist of the following story.

A man was traveling in a boat. The cool waters, green trees swaying on the banks, the twittering of the birds, and the gentle breeze enchanted him, and he was absorbed in the beauty of the place. He allowed the boat to float of its own accord, along with the flow of the river. He never bothered about at the direction in which the boat was going. As the boat was floating effortlessly, he did not have to use the oars. It was very comfortable to sail in the boat without any exertion and he was very happy.

After a while, the wind rose and the boat began to move faster. The lazy fellow was now overjoyed. "Oh, wow! I am sailing really fast!" he exulted. A little later, there was a distant roar. "Great, now nature is playing an orchestra for me".

Suddenly the boat began to move uncontrollably towards a waterfall. Once he realized the gravity of the situation, he tried to control the boat with his oars, but it was too late. He could not prevent himself from floundering in the churning waters below.

The lethargic mentality of this person can be called "Niagara Syndrome."

If you don't plan, you will perish. Don't allow your life to come to the edge of the Niagra falls before you decide to change course, be it about health, relationships, family, business, or education. Don't be blown by your unintelligent logic. Here is an example:

Friend : What is your age?

Mullah : I don't know.

Friend :Why?

Mullah : It is constantly changing, day-by-day.

Reflections

Yoga of Wisdom

Plan or Perish

Yoga of Action

Plan purposefully. Prepare prayerfully.
Proceed positively. Pursue persistently.

Contemplation

Fear not tomorrow. God, the Almighty is already there.

Be thankful if your work is a little harder than you want. A knife can't be sharpened on a piece of velvet.

Be grateful for what you have and not sad for what you don't have.

Be a possibility thinker.

If you don't plan, you will perish.

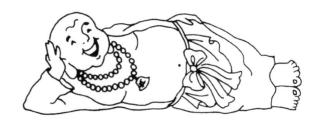

VISION 1...2...3...

A fisherman went to sell fish in a crowded market. He was going to this market the first time. He chose a place by the side of a compound wall. He put up a board that read "Fresh Fish Sold Here". Standing back, he viewed his own handiwork, checked if everything was okay. He read what he wrote once again.

Now, he thought to himself, "Would any one sell stale fish? Then why should I use the word "fresh"?" He erased the word "fresh."

The board read "Fish Sold Here." When he saw the signboard again, he wondered, "Have I brought the fish to donate it? It is well understood that I am going to sell it", so he erased "sold" too. Now the signboard read, "Fish Here." Looking intently at the signboard, he began to laugh. It was obvious that the fish

was here and not somewhere else! So why the word "here"?"
And he removed that word also.

Now all that remained on the signboard was the word "Fish."
The man took one last look at the signboard and thought,
"Anyone who comes to the market can identify this place by
the very smell of fresh fish. As soon as they see the fish, they
will recognize it. There is no doubt about that. Then why use
that word? He erased the word "Fish". Now the signboard was
blank and empty!

All our problems are like the signboard of the fisherman. Once
we learn to view the problems in the right perspective, our
problems too will disappear. But the saddest part is that most of
us do not even know how to view things!

The word for philosophy in Sanskrit, *"darshan"*, literally means
vision. It means "seeing." What are the things necessary for
seeing? Is it enough to have eyes? "No, eyes alone are not
enough, one must have awareness", says Lord Krishna.

Only when we have awareness shall we know how to discern
differences between things, people and ourselves.

"How many houses do you own? What is the market value?
Which car do you use?"

We ask such questions while we talk about material objects/ things. Things must be viewed mathematically. Things must be viewed as tools and used as tools!

Next, how do we see human beings? One cannot measure human beings with the same yardstick that we use for things. "Affectionate father, loving mother, dear sister, and grateful friend" We use attributes such as these to characterize people; we use yardsticks like love, affection and relationship.

But in reality, what do we do?

Relationships are assessed on the basis of their instrumental value. Persons who we should love - mother, father, brother, children, friends -- are used as tools. Things should be seen mathematically and people should be seen with love. Right.

How should we see ourselves? In order to understand how we see ourselves, first we must understand what we mean by "WE."

There are three dimensions to our bodies: the *material body* made of flesh and bones; the *energy body*, made of our knowledge, thoughts, and mind, and *"awareness"* or *"shakti"*- in Sanskrit."

Can you see how we are now back at our starting point?

In order to face problems, what we need is "Objective Vision"; and in order to visualize something, we need "Awareness."

It is wrong on our part to think that we should not have problems. The only place where there can be no problem is the graveyard. That is to say, only the dead are devoid of problems. All those alive would surely have problems. If there were no problems, then life itself would be dull.

Tripping, getting hurt, suffering pain, chasing victory with pain, one's moment of glory being snatched away by some one else -- all these things happen not as much in life as in football. But a true champion considers every problem as a challenge.

When a football player kicks the ball towards the goal, if the goalkeeper and the players of the opposite team remain idle, without offering any resistance, would that game become exciting? Would that game be interesting to players? Or would anyone be interested in watching such a game at all? Reflect on this for a moment.

Learn to enjoy every problem in life. Keep your ability to enjoy the challenge above your problem. Create waves of joy wherever you go.

Reflections

Yoga of Wisdom

Treat problem as an opportunity to grow

Yoga of Action

Act with a commitment that every problem contains within itself the ingredients of solution.

Contemplation

Think of doubt as an invitation welcoming you to think.

Man loves objects and uses people instead of loving people and using objects.

Only dead people don't have problems.

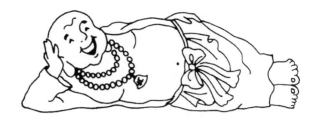

AN ORACLE... AND A MIRACLE

I was talking about problems.

One type is external, beyond our control; the other is internal, which we inflict on ourselves by choice. The main cause for this is greed.

A Zen Monk went to a small village. The villagers gathered around him and pleaded, "Please help us get rid of our problems; let our desires be fulfilled, so that our lives will be full of joy." The monk listened to them, silently. The next day, he arranged for a divine sound to speak to them thus, "Tomorrow at mid-day, a miracle is going to take place in this village. Pack all your problems in an imaginary sack, take it across the river and empty the sack there. Then, in the same imaginary sack, put everything that you want --gold, jewellery, food, whatever -- and take it home. All your desires will be met."

The villagers doubted whether this oracle was true or not. However, the voice from the heaven astounded them. They thought they had nothing to lose by following the instructions. If it were true, then they would really get what they wanted, and if it were false, any way, they wouldn't be worse off. So they decided to do as they were told .

Next day, at noon, they packed their troubles in an imaginary sack and went across the river, emptied it there and brought back all that they thought would bring them happiness --gold, car, house, jewellery, diamonds.

On their return, they were really taken aback! Whatever the oracle had said had come true! The man who wanted a car found one parked in front of his house. The one who wished for a palatial house found that his hut had turned into one. They were all so happy! Their joy knew no bounds!

But alas! The joy and celebration lasted only for a while. Soon they began to compare themselves with their neighbors. Each one felt that the person next door was happier and richer than himself. Now they began to grumble to themselves, "I asked for a simple chain, while the girl next door asked for an ornate gold necklace and got it! I just asked for a house but the man residing opposite asked for a mansion. I too should have asked for such things! It was a wonderful opportunity, the chance of a lifetime, but I let it slip by".

Such were the thoughts that occupied their minds. They returned to the monk and piled their complaints in front of him. The village was once again plunged into frustration. Many feel that they cannot be happy if they have problems. I wish to counsel them. Do not link your happiness to problems. Problems there will be in everybody's life. Tell yourself "Let there be problems, but I shall still continue to be happy and cheerful." This does not mean that one should not think of finding solutions to problems.

Who has faced more problems than Lord Krishna? Wasn't his uncle Kamsa plotting to kill him while he was still in his mother's womb? In the Mahabharata war, he served as the charioteer of Arjuna. Did Arjuna not create problems at the last minute by casting off his armor and declining to fight? In the battlefield of Kurukshetra, each day was fraught with problems of all kinds. Each arrow that was aimed at Arjuna whizzed past Krishna's head! Despite all this, the joyful smile always adorned his face!

Lord Krishna instructs us thus: "Learn to view sorrow and joy as equal; be open to joy, be open to sorrow. They are two sides of the same coin. Try to learn from both, and clarity will emerge. This clarity will bring you bliss."

Reflections

Yoga of Wisdom

*An untrained mind creates its own
prison of unhappiness*

Yoga of Action

*Dis-identify with an unhappy mind and treasure your
experiences.*

DULL MOVIE... DISLIKED SCENES...!

Recently I was in Hyderabad to conduct the "LIFE Program." For some of the participants memories of certain painful experiences of their past still remained as deep wounds in their hearts, and kept coming back to ruin their present.

Such memories are painful and depressing. How can we escape them?

Usually, participants in LIFE share their inner traumas. I encourage them to speak frankly about memories that remain as festering wounds.

One person's story was as follows: My friend and I got together and started a construction company. Since I was in government service, I ran the firm in my friend's name. Very soon the business prospered. In order to concentrate on the work, I even resigned from my government job. Sometime later, for the purpose of filing income tax returns, I asked my friend for the account books of the company. And he said, "Look, for the work that you are doing, take whatever pay you want. But don't come here asking about accounts and so on." His words literally burned my whole being.

I had given him the entire responsibility of running the company including signing powers, fully trusting him. Now I was helpless! This was the company I had started by investing all that I had, including the money I got by selling the family jewels. I simply wiped the tears of frustration from my eyes and walked out. The results of years of toil and sweat were snatched from me in a trice. This happened many years ago. Later I started another construction company, which is quite profitable now. Yet, the treachery of my friend still makes me feel sad and bitter.

Next a young woman came forward to speak. She said, "I fell in love with a man and married him. But from the beginning, my mother-in-law looked down on me with hostility. Within a few weeks of our marriage, my sister-in-law was widowed in an accident. My mother-in-law began cursing me as the cause of the accident. When my relatives came to express their condolences, she chided me in their presence saying, "You are a harbinger of bad luck! The moment you stepped into the house, the tragedy took place. You don't have a place here, get out at once"

On the same day, my husband and I left the house. After a few years, my younger brother-in-law got married. Though my husband was the eldest son of the family, he was not invited for the wedding. Later on, my father-in-law turned seriously ill. We visited him. Even on his deathbed, his anger towards me had not abated.

My mother-in-law said, "You are a monster who brings bad luck! If even the air around you touches my husband, he will die! So, get out!" As soon as we returned home, my father-in-law passed away, and my husband, who was his first-born child, did not even have the opportunity to see his face before he was cremated!

"Many years have passed since, and I have been living here in Hyderabad, several hundred kilometers away from the town where my mother-in-law stays. We are fairly comfortable, blessed with children and prosperity. Yet, every time I remember the insults heaped on me especially on my husband, my heart aches cruelty to it all! What shall I do?" Instead of answering them individually, I told them, "There are several such stories of hurt and agony. Give me the name of a boring movie, the one that you hate the most!"

Each named one movie or another. I asked them to get that movie from a video parlor and watch it all through the night, again and again.

"Oh, no! I cannot do that! I would die of boredom. Tell me something that I can do", they all pleaded.

"Well, the treachery of friends, ill-treatment by your mother-in-law -- these are also painful scenes that you dislike immensely. Why do you insist on playing and replaying them over and over again on your mind's screen? If you refuse to watch a film based on fiction because you find it boring, why do you want replay the scenes that you loathe in your mind? Allow yourself to forget them. The wound will heal and the scar vanish by itself", I said.

The reason why small children are always happy is that they do not carry burdens from the past...they forget painful incidents quickly, but they harp on joyful experiences again and again and enjoy them. We too should learn to be like children. That would considerably lessen the burden that we carry in our hearts.

To put all this in a nutshell, the past must only tutor us, not torture us!

Then a hidden intelligence will surface, which will guide us in mysterious ways.

Reflections

Yoga of Wisdom

*Transform your Mind and
Transcend Unhappiness*

Yoga of Action

*Learn from the Past, Rejoice the Present,
Plan for the Future.*

Contemplation

Very few people live. Most of us are committing suicide by unwisely desiring.

Hope for the best and accept the worst.

Joy is not the absence of problems.

There are certain flowers that will not yield their fragrance untill they are crushed.

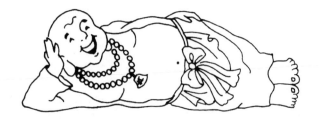

AN ARMOUR AROUND THE BODY

There are several instances of joy and happiness in every one's life. Every time your heart feels heavy, please remind yourself of those happy moments, again and again. Then you will forget your feelings of hurt and will be wafted on the wings of happy memories. This technique is known as "Super-imposing technique."

This is a story about a lady from a very prosperous family.

It was her birthday. When she woke up in the morning, she could scarcely believe her eyes. Her room was decorated with colorful balloons and glittering papers. During the previous night, her husband had taken the trouble to decorate her room to celebrate her birthday. He had done the work silently, with total care and love. When she learnt of this, she could not contain her joy. She hugged him to show her gratitude and affection.

Now, she came out of her room. Her parents, who lived hundreds of miles away, arrived on a surprise visit. Her only child presented her with a gift. All this made her as happy as she had never been before!

She wore a new silk sari presented by her husband for the special occasion and went to a temple with the family. In the temple her new Sari was stained by the oil used for lighting lamps.

That was all it took to drive her to depression, and make her forget the joy she had been experiencing the whole morning. She was so obsessed with the stain that it was as if the oil had seeped into her very soul, blotting out everything else. Later, to assuage her feelings, her husband took her out, bought her expensive gifts and they saw a film and dined out. She could, however, not forget the oil stain. The thoughts of the oil stain tormented her throughout that day!

What happened was that one unwelcome event cast its shadow, or imposed itself over a series of happy occurrences. My question is, "Can't we reverse the situation?" My answer is, "Yes, we can."

We have already talked about people who *hurt* others by their words. Just think for a moment about the type of people who *get hurt* by such words. Usually, words and actions of others normally affect only people with a low energy level. When a one's energy level is high, no one can hurt him/her.

Think of the moments in your life when you were at the peak of your energy levels. It may be the day you passed your final examination, or the day you got a job or your sweetheart accepted your proposal.

If your energy level is at its peak, sharp words aimed at you won't hurt you one bit.

So try to imagine that every moment of your life is like the moment when your girlfriend said "I love you!" and continue to be cheerful always. The energy field that forms around your body will then act like an armor protecting you from the invectives of others.

This energy field is not a piece of fiction as some may allege. Every person has an aura, either positive or negative, around him/her. This has been revealed by Kirlan photography.

Reflections

Yoga of Wisdom

Learn to see the tricks of your Mind

Yoga of Action

Learn to feel Silence and you will hear the Divine answer. Two people cannot hate each other if there is silence.

SPRING OF ENERGY

How can you strengthen your energy field and maintain enthusiasm at an optimum level?

Hindu scriptures talk of *"drishti, shrushti,* and *vaada". drishti* means "vision", *shrushti* "creation", and *"vaada"* "dialogue".

What we see becomes the creation. We become whatever we envision ourselves to be. More specifically, we gradually metamorphose into whatever we see ourselves to be. Chant to yourself, "I am full of energy and spirits." Believe in what you say, and you will surely remain full of energy. Does it seem to be impractical? Have a look at this example.

A young man woke up early in the morning after a good sleep, and completed his regular exercises. He dressed and set out for work. His neighbor, who always accompanied him, asked with great concern, "You seem to be off color today. Are you not keeping well?"

Next, he met a friend at the street corner. He too observed, "What is wrong? You look terribly out of sorts today."

The young man entered the office and the receptionist also enquired, "Oh, you don't look well. Why don't you take a day off?" By now, the young man really began to feel sick. So he took a day off from office and returned home.

This is not a piece of fiction. It was an experiment conducted on him without his knowledge to observe the influence of mind over matter.

This exemplifies the way our thoughts affect our body. At times, it works the other way too: our body affects our thoughts.

Consider some people's habit of chewing on their nails under tension. Once the habit gets ingrained, tension will arise in the mind even if the nail is bitten in normal course. Some persons sit with their jaw resting on their hand when they feel dull. Even if they happen to sit casually like that, they would begin to feel dull for no reason at all.

You may all have witnessed "fire-walking" during temple festivals. Those devotees who participate in fire walking may not be professionals. Yet, the moment they decide to "fire-walk", they imbibe the enthusiasm of the veterans. From where do they get this? From their minds of course! (Please do not try this on your own: supervision by experienced fire - walkers is necessary for proper execution of this spiritual feat.)

Most of the ideas discussed here are already known to all of us. Still, we are unable to pull ourselves out of depression. We simply drown in our sorrows. Why do we do so?

Most of us are more particular about making a point than about being happy. Being happy is not our first priority.

An aristocratic gentleman known to me owns a big house in a central locality in Bangalore. If he were to just sell the small out-house adjacent to the main house, he would make at least half a million dollars. With that money, he could live royally. But his point of view is that an ancestral inheritance should never be sold.

So, what is his situation today? Though he lives in a big house, he struggles to pay the property tax, telephone bill, electricity bill etc., as there is no income from his ancestral inheritance. A real pity!

Some go to the extreme of committing suicide in order to prove their point of view.

We must consider happiness to be more important than our beliefs. What is the problem as long as our happiness and contentment are obtained through just means? Once we cultivate this attitude, there will be no dearth of energy or enthusiasm in our lives!

Reflections

Yoga of Wisdom

Allow enthusiasm to grow and prosper in your acre of diamonds.

Yoga of Action

Sing a song of enthusiasm and create magic around it.

SING, DANCE, LAUGH AND CRY!

Quite some time back, I was in Hyderabad to talk on imagination and creativity. The number of participants was very small, quite unusual for my talks. When I sought the reason, I was told that people were interested in issues of practical life. They were under the impression that imagination and creativity were concerns only of painters, poets, writers, and artists, not of ordinary people. Nothing could be more wrong! Take the case of toothpaste. Advertisers cite so many attributes of various brands; "strengthens gums", "stops bad breath", "kills germs", "removes plaques", "mint-flavored", "more foamy", "specially made for children" "irresistible to the opposite sex!"

Imagination is essential not only for those who are involved in the arts, advertising, or trade and business, but also for government employees, housewives, students, retired persons.

Recently I met a young girl in Madras during one of my "LIFE Programs." Her parents lived in a small town near Thanjavur. She was a skilled artist. She stayed with her aunt in Madras who ran an Arts & Crafts school. She was learning how to manage the school. Her aunt showered her with love and treated her as one of her own daughters. The problem arose when the young girl happened to talk to men who visited the school; the aunt felt upset and scolded her.

"I am an educated girl. I know what is good and what is bad for me. When I converse with men who come here, I stick to professional matters. No man can cheat me. So please don't get worried", the girl explained clearly to her aunt many times, requesting her to avoid getting tense. Her words had no effect whatsoever on her aunt.

"Now, what do I do? No matter how I explain my stand, gently, or in anger, nothing seems to work. How do I make her understand the situation?", the girl asked.

Though she was imaginative enough to create paintings and pictures, she found it impossible to make her aunt understand something that she considered right and proper. Here, she had failed to use her imagination effectively.

I initiated a small role-play, with the girl as the aunt and myself as the girl. From that she drew many ideas on how to reassure her aunt and make her see her point of view.

In our lives, we encounter many people who prove quite irksome. The next-door neighbor who insists on playing music at full volume; the men across the street who regularly dump their garbage in front of our gates; the quarrelsome wife; nagging husband; disobedient kids. If we are to handle all these, we cannot employ just one common method. If we consider them as challenges to our creative ability, we may find hundreds of ways to handle the situations!

Recall the kindergarten story of the thirsty crow. It is all about creativity. The thirsty crow, tired after searching for water, finally finds a little water at the bottom of a tall jar. It then drops pebbles into the jar to raise the level of the water. If this is not creativity, what else is?

There are certain basic necessities for the growth of creative thinking.

Our brain can be divided into four parts. While we think rationally, the logical part of the brain functions. While planning, the second part works. The third part of the brain has to do with intuition. This is related to what we call "gut-feeling". The fourth part of the brain is the seat of emotions, i.e., happiness, sorrow, etc.

Generally, men use the logic and planning side of the brain more often. So, for them the first two parts of the brain are more functional. Women are highly emotional. Thus, intuitive and emotive parts of the brain, i.e., the third and fourth regions are more active in women.

We need to use all the four parts equally in order to be fully effective. Many of us cannot accept that we can and should laugh out loud, cry freely, sing, dance, run or jump. What would be the result of this approach? The fourth part of the brain would remain unused and thus become dysfunctional. This is not healthy. Only by using all the four parts can we become complete human beings. Our brains would then function to their full capacities. This understanding is necessary for the full blossoming of our creative imagination.

So, while you are reading a really good and humorous book, laugh loudly. If you feel sad, cry without restraint, in privacy of course. If you feel happy, sing aloud and dance around, if you wish! There is nothing to be ashamed about in dancing. Lord Shiva, whom we worship as the supreme God - Parameshwara is none other than Nataraja, the King of Dance! A dancing deity.

Reflections

Yoga of Wisdom

*Being creative is to respect
the creator in you.*

Yoga of Action

*Give yourself a break and
start seeing things differently.*

Contemplation

Better be with enlightened people in prison than fools in paradise.

Education means destroying the problematic mind and not stuffing the memory.

Imagination is more important than knowledge.

.. Albert Einstein.

Imagination, inspiration and commitment to excel is the mother of creativity.

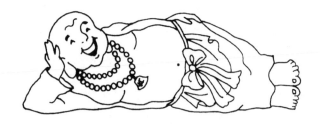

A WITCH WITHIN OUR MIND!

Some of you may have heard with the story of Rapunzel. She was a beautiful child. When she was very young, a witch took her away from her parents and imprisoned her in a tall tower, deep inside a dense forest. The tower had no doors or stairs. At the very top, there was one window. Rapunzel eventually grew into a beauty, her skin the color of roses and long hair like spun gold.

Rapunzel grew up knowing nothing about the outside world. The witch used to visit her through a window, climbing by grasping her long hair. But the witch never told her how beautiful she was. She was very possessive of Rapunzel and did not want her to leave the tower. She thought that if Rapunzel learnt of her true nature, or of the world outside, she would escape from her and go away. There was nothing in the tower that could reflect anything; so the girl had never even seen her own face. All her contact was with the witch.

The witch constantly told Rapunzel how ugly she was, and insulted her always. Rapunzel had no choice but to believe all this. She used to feel sad that God had created her ugly and cried bitterly, all day long.

One fine day, a prince happened to come to the forest to hunt. Having lost his way, he chanced by the tall tower, where he glimpsed the fair face of Rapunzel and fell in love with her immediately. He climbed to the top of the tower, just the same way that the witch used to, using the girl's long hair. He told her that she was exceedingly beautiful, and that he loved her dearly.

For the first time in her life, Rapunzel realized how good-looking she was. Thereafter, they met often and their love grew deep and strong. The story ends, after many mishaps, with the prince releasing Rapunzel from the prison and marrying her. And, as in all fairy tales, they lived happily ever after!

Now, you may wonder why I had to relate this fairy tale here! Before we go into an analysis of that, let us remind ourselves of the ideas on creativity we shared earlier.

A boy was studying in primary school. For some reason, he was unable to score good marks in English. His family members as well the teachers at school told him repeatedly that he was no good in English. He faced this criticism all through his school and college days.

Now, is there any difference between this and what the witch got Rapunzel to believe? This is known as "Negative Belief."

There is a witch in us- "Negative Belief." There is a prince in us; "Creativity." Our mind, if it becomes repetitive, can be a prison in which the beautiful Rapunzel would be trapped.

This young boy, just like Rapunzel, took what others told him as the whole truth and nothing but the truth. He even avoided reading English newspapers and magazines. He refused to speak even a few words in English. If at all he faced a situation where he was forced to speak in English, he would slip away under some pretext.

This way of frequently telling the same thing to oneself is known as "Repetitive Thinking." The tower represents repetitive thinking.

It is like a pair of oxen bound to a wooden log in an oil-mill, moving in the same track again and again. Just as Rapunzel was imprisoned in a tall tower, this young man was imprisoned by his own repetitive thinking. As a result, he never even attempted to learn English.

To develop this boy's self confidence, a prince must come along. That prince is what I call "Creativity." Only this prince can overcome the witch that is "Negative Belief." The prince - "Creativity" alone can release the princess -"Ability" from the prison of "Repetitive Thinking."

Feeling shy about speaking in English is only one such example! Life is replete with many such examples. We come across a prejudiced boss, a debtor who refuses to repay the loan, or a spouse who is always rude. If we think that such characters never change, we cannot find any solution to our problems. In order to plan our approach to them, we have to think clearly; the most essential tool for all of us is "creativity."

Well, what is it that blocks creativity in us?

One main impediment to imaginative thinking is a "Repetitive Mind." This is what prevents us from viewing any issue from a totally new perspective. The bound-to-the-oil-mill -oxen are the block!

Reflections

Yoga of Wisdom

A repetitive mind is a psychological prison.

Yoga of Action

Creatively dig into new ideas and create your own beautiful World.

Contemplation

Acting on a good idea is better than having a good idea.

.. *Robert Half.*

The most difficult things to open are a closed mind and heart.

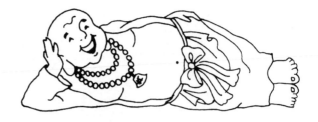

WHO GETS THE PIECE OF CAKE?

There are people slumbering all the time to beat what they call boredom.

Particularly during school and collage holidays, one can hear the refrain "It is so boring to sit at home!" Well, what does boredom mean? To put it simply, boredom is what we feel when we are doing things we don't enjoy doing, like sitting idle, rolling on bed, talking to people we don't like etc.

When we do things that we enjoy, life is not boring. But many of us fail to understand this simple fact. Even if work we enjoy doing is available, we postpone embarking on it.

If there is something you enjoy doing, do not postpone it! There is a humorous story that exemplifies the idea.

An Englishman, an Arab and an Indian were together. They found a small piece of cake, a rare delicacy in that region. It was too small to be shared amongst the three of them.

So, they came to a consensus. They would put the piece of cake in a container and go to sleep. And whoever saw the best dream could have the cake. With this decision, they all went to sleep.

Next morning, they all met to share their dreams. First the Englishman said, "Last night, God appeared in my dream. He took me to the Garden of Eden and showed me lots of wonderful things". Next the Arab said, "God appeared in my dream also. But I took Him to my garden and showed Him all the Arabian delights."

It was the Indian's turn to speak. He said, "God appeared in my dream too! But we did not go to any garden. He only looked at me and said, "You fool! With such a delicious piece of cake right in front of you, you are lying down and dreaming! Get up at once and eat that cake!" How could I disobey Him? So I got up and ate the cake."

The other two opened the container and found that the cake was missing!

Let us take the message from this story.

Do not postpone being happy.

If any activity gives us great joy, don't postpone doing it.

One can slightly modify this sentence to read, "Whatever you do, do it with joy and total involvement." Then the very word "boredom" will disappear from your dictionary.

If you do not know swimming, then go and learn how to swim. If you have never gone boating, then do that. Master a musical instrument. Try to learn a new language. If you find all this too cumbersome, then at least go and meet a friend you have not seen for years! This will help you overcome boredom.

A Zen monk was on his deathbed. All his disciples thronged around him in sorrow. They asked, "Master! What is your last message for us?"

The monk, instead of replying to their question, asked for a sweet. When the sweet was brought, he looked at it with joy, like a small child. He then ate it, bit by bit, fully savouring its taste, tapping his hands rhythmically. Then, he simply died. Eating a sweet is a very ordinary affair, but even that should be done with total involvement and relish. This was the last message that the monk wished to convey.

It is not only those who sit idle at home that feel bored. Those who do one and the same thing for years like the oxen tethered to the oil mill can also feel bored.

Every human being has four dimensions in life - Intimate life, Family life, Professional life and Social life. A person has to live in all these dimensions.

Supposing our living room, bedroom and kitchen are all clean, but the toilet is unattended. What would happen? The foul smell from it would ruin the atmosphere of other rooms that are kept clean! Similarly, even if one of the four dimensions of our life were unfulfilled and empty, it would make the whole life inadequate and meaningless.

Treat life holistically. Learn to create a balance among all aspects of life. Don't get lost in one aspect of life and neglect the other. For one will start affecting the other.

Reflections

Yoga of Wisdom

Learn to enjoy little things; there are many of them.

Yoga of Action

Enjoy yourself and enjoy today.
Do not waste time by grieving over a bad yesterday.
Who knows, tomorrow may not be
as good as today.

Contemplation

Do not postpone being happy.

Our prayers are so often mechanical.

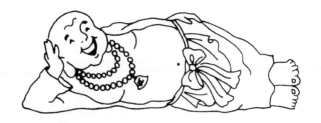

OH, GOD!

We pray to God. But most often, what is the quality of our prayers?

"My wife is a nag. Please change her character. My children are not obedient. Change their behavior. The next-door neighbor is a brute. He is always quarrelling with me for nothing, please change his ways."

We keep pestering God to change others around us. To put it in another way, we are actually saying, "God, you are not doing anything about all these. Please change yourself! Change yourself from being idle and do something favorable to me."

Can you see how strange all this is?

Do we pray to change ourselves or to change God?

We know that prayer is not meant to change God, but we persist in our foolishness.

There are others who declare proudly to every one they meet, "I offer prayers for an hour every day without fail, come rain or shine." For them, even wearing the sacred ash is a matter of image. They are bound to the ritual of prayer, they don't savor its spirit.

There is yet another kind of prayer.

A lady seated at a window was watching the scene outside. The mountain ranges at distance were pretty. Suddenly she remembered a proverb "Prayers can move mountains." She wanted to test God. Closing her eyes, she knelt on the floor and prayed, "God, if you move the mountain between the sea and my house, I would get the sea breeze. So please move the mountain." When she opened her eyes, she saw that the mountain had not moved an inch. She smiled and said, "I was very sure that the mountain would not move. The saying that prayers can move mountains is all baloney. My hunch was correct."

She prayed with the conviction that prayer would not move the mountain. The essence of the prayer came from disbelief rather than belief. Here, prayer was a mere ritual and not an expression of commitment.

There is another kind of prayer, viz., prayer for its own sake – a mechanical observance. The mind wanders all over even as the lips part to let out the chant.

A member of a church performed great services to humanity. The Head of the Church presented him with a miraculous horse in appreciation of his services.

That horse was very pious. If the rider said, "Oh God", the horse would run very fast. If one wanted the horse to keep running, one had to say," Oh God" twice. Similarly, if the rider wanted to bring the horse to a halt, he had to say, "Thank you, God."

The Head of the Church explained the language of the horse, and bade farewell. The disciple mounted the newly acquired horse and said "Oh God." The horse galloped. The disciple felt as though he were flying. Highly excited, he said, "Oh God, Oh God." The horse galloped as fast as the wind on the mountain. The disciple, who was earlier so exulted with the ride, was afraid now. The horse was racing towards a steep cliff. He tried in vain to hold back the reins to stop it. But the horse kept running. Suddenly he recalled the words of the Bishop, and, with his eyes closed, he screamed, "Thank you, God." His voice echoed over the mountain range, and the horse stopped at once. The disciple opened his eyes and looked around. He froze in horror as he noticed that he was at the very edge of the precipice. Thinking how he had escaped a great danger, he sighed "Oh God."

This story shows how mechanically we recite the name of God, and how we pray without fully knowing its real significance.

How do we pray? The answers can be found in the life of Kabir. Kabir says:

There was not a place left where I did not seek God. Temples, tanks, towers, all over the place I roamed looking for God. I could not find Him." Finally exhausted, I said to myself, "So what if I cannot find God? Let me consider myself as a God-realized person and let me experience Him." I began to live as loving, as silent and as blissful as God. Godliness came into me of its own accord. Lo, the miracle happened. I heard God calling me "Kabir, Kabir, where are you? I am searching for you."

Kabir said, "All along I was searching for you, Oh God; but now you have come looking for me. I have realized the God within me and hence, I have no more business with an external God."

Modern psychology calls this an "Act-As-If Theory." At the center of this theory is "trust." Trust in the fact that you are blissful, silent and loving. This trust creates divine magic.

If you do not find what you are seeking, trust that you have already found it, and act accordingly. Then you will surely find it! This is how the mystery of prayer works.

Reflections

Yoga of Wisdom

*Mystery of prayer is magical.
Just trust it.*

Yoga of Action

*Trust is the essence to
understand mystery.*

A BOOST TO ENTHUSIASM!

Swamiji! All around me there are packs of howling jackals. Business associates, family members and friends all betrayed me one after another. My heart aches to think of all the loss, misery and shame I have suffered. I am unable to make out what I am carrying on my shoulders, whether it is my head or a heavy boulder. My brain is fraught with worries. How do I escape this?

All I can say is the following.

If your problems are solved through worrying, please go ahead and worry. Do you know what happens when you worry all the time? Worry is like a small stone that grows into a huge granite boulder. All through the time you worry, your failures, insults, pains and sorrows parade in front of your eyes, in succession.

Worry is like a rocking chair; it gives you a feeling of movement, but takes you nowhere.

On the other hand, if you are happy, the fruits of your labor, your success stories, happy moments you're your achievements play on your mental screen.

Now tell me! When does your capacity reach its maximum? When you are worried, or when you are happy? Only when you are happy, right?

All right! How to be happy? The first recipe for happiness is laughter. One should laugh heartily, laugh until your muscles tire!

You might have heard of the "Laughing Buddha." There were three Buddhist monks. Just as Buddha got enlightenment under the Bodhi tree, these three monks got enlightenment through laughter. They later taught the world that laughing could be a way of meditation. They called it laughing meditation. They spread the message of laughter all their life.

One of the monks passed away. The other two sat on either side of his body and began to laugh. The townspeople were angered by this inappropriate behavior and started abusing them. The monks told them, "Our friend spent his whole life helping people to understand the message of laughter. We are laughing because

- he has won the game of death first

- the message from his life was laughter

- if we do not bid him farewell with laughter, his soul will laugh at us that we are trapped by seriousness like so many others.

So, we are laughing, according to his last wish."

It was time to conduct the funeral rites. The monk had said before his death, "Since I was laughing throughout my life, laughter has cleansed all impurities from within me. So please do not wash my body with water."

Accordingly, his body was not bathed, but taken directly to the funeral pyre. As the body caught fire, there was a burst of crackers from the pyre. Yes! The monk had fastened crackers to his body under his flowing robes before his death. He had done so to make every one laugh even after his death! Hence the name the "Laughing Buddha."

Apply any amount of cosmetics if you wish to; face powder, eye shadow, and lipstick to enhance your beauty, but would they ever be equal to one genuine smile? There is no better beauty aid than a genuine smile!

Laughter is a tonic that develops acquaintance to friendship. Not only does laughter fetch you new friends, it also strengthens old ones.

"Laugh aloud and your disease will disappear", so goes Tamil proverb. Today, hospitals in USA are beginning to realize the truth of this proverb! Some hospitals have Humor Nurses whose job is to make their patients laugh.

Whenever feelings of anger, sadness, or lethargy strike, read a good joke and laugh heartily! Do not complain that the joke is not good enough to invoke a hearty laugh. Simply use a joke as an excuse to laugh. When one laughs, certain chemical changes take place in the body. These changes dissolve all negative feelings such as anger, sorrow and depression. You would feel totally refreshed, as if you had just bathed in a waterfall cascading from the top of a mountain: and the body would be rejuvenated!

Reflections

Yoga of Wisdom

*Life lived happily is the measure
of a successful life.*

Yoga of Action

*Discover the treasure of happiness within.
Happiness is the result of not investing in misery.*

Contemplation

We get a word, lose its meaning and thereby miss the context.

An unwise person empties his head every time he opens his mouth.

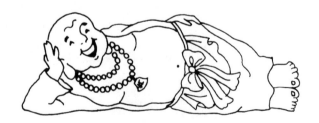

THE DANCE OF NATARAJA!

Many people smoke. Some drink.

If you asked them why they smoke or drink, they would reply that it helps them overcome their boredom or forget their worries. Whenever their body or mind feels depressed or dull, or when they feel stressed, they wish to change that state. In order to do that, they resort to smoking or drinking.

When the mental or physical rhythm remains static for long i.e., within the same wavelength, boredom results. Then lethargy is sure to set in. Sometimes, a sense of depression also may engulf a person. This kind of situation does not make anyone happy. So they think if there were some change in the mental or physical rhythm, that would create some joy, some enthusiasm. Thus they surrender themselves to cigarettes and liquor.

There is no doubt that cigarettes and liquor change biorhythms. But, at the same time, they also lead to some bad side effects. Don't they?

Is there anything that could change the body rhythm and infuse enthusiasm without any bad side effects?

Yes, there is! Surely there is!

One such important activity is dance.

Now, don't frown, saying, "What? Dance?"

Don't turn away saying that dance is something not appropriate to our culture. In fact, our culture and dance are intricately interwoven! Bharata Natyam, Kuchipudi, Odissi, Mohini Aattam, and Yakshagana are a few of the multifarious dance forms that arose and flourished in our country.

The word "Hindu" has many meanings. One of the important meanings is "It is that which destroys something that keeps us low."

What is it that deprives us of our enthusiasm, excitement, energy and self-confidence?

Laziness, self-pity, depression and other similar feelings. Don't you agree? First, we must destroy these negative feelings.

Just look at the idol of Lord Nataraja.

The demon under the feet of the dancing Nataraja represents the powers that take away positive energies from us. The dancing Lord holds a flame in one of his four hands - it represents the fire of understanding. The saffron robes worn by the Saints (who have renounced the world) also depict the same – the fire – the fire of knowledge.

The drum held in another hand by Nataraja signifies waves of ecstasy, an emotion that accompanies enlightenment.

The third hand of Nataraja shows a conch that declares "Live Life Fearlessly."

The fourth hand of Nataraja points towards the feet of the Lord, representing surrender of the self. To live fearlessly is possible if one knows the value of surrender.

What and where to surrender?

Ego. Surrender your ego at the feet of the Lord.

If we destroy the demon that pulls us down, we get into gamboling enthusiasm. This enthusiasm leads to happiness.

At this juncture, I am reminded of a nursery rhyme taught to tiny tots. The rhyme goes like this:

What time is it?

It is the time to be "happy"

The time to be happy is "now"

The place to be happy is "here"

The way to be happy is to "make some one happy and create a heaven right here".

There is a particular type of dance known as "Sufi Dance." The steps and movements of this dance are choreographed to simulate motions that seem to discard all the problems that we have. The end of the dance symbolizes giving the joy flowing out of our hearts to every one, like Santa Claus does.

Now you may well ask me, "Swamiji! You say that dancing would change the body rhythm, which would make enthusiasm spring forth. In that case, what is the difference between dances performed in discotheques and the dance of Nataraja?"

In a disco when you dance, your *sex* center is activated and you dance only for fun. In meditative dance, your *bliss* center is activated. Dance becomes an expression of joy.

But if we dance like Lord Nataraja, with mastery over our base emotions, i.e., the demon, then the dancer disappears, and only the dance remains. Such a dance is a dance born out of ecstasy, a forgotten language.

Well, how do we dance like that?

If you dance *for* happiness, you will not get happiness. So at the outset, dance *with* happiness. That is to say, do not dance with happiness as the destination. Instead, dance with dance as the source of your happiness.

Reflections

Yoga of Wisdom

*Understand bliss by treating each day
like as if it were the first day of your honeymoon
and the last day of your vacation.*

Yoga of Action

Keep your mind empty and let joy find you.

Contemplation

The worst boss anyone can have is a bad habit.

Habits are either the best of servants or the worst of masters.
Develop a habit to be happy & pure.

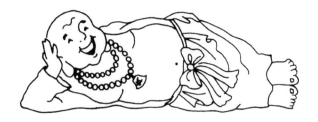

WHAT ARE YOU –
SIEVE OR WINNOW?

A disciple asked his Master –

What is the power that makes the eyes see?

"The eye of the eye!"

What is the power that makes the ears hear?

"The ear of the ear!"

The Master then asked the disciple – "Did you understand what I said?"

"No, I did not!" said the disciple in confusion.

"If you did not understand my explanation, it means you have understood.

If you have understood, it means you have not understood!"

Do you think that the above dialogue is between people under the influence of narcotics?

Well, the above dialogue is found in Kena Upanishad, one of the Hindu Scriptures!

Human beings possess one special faculty that none of the other living beings have, viz, the ability to think. A computer on the ground controls a satellite thousands of kilometers away. It can carry out all the instructions set by humans, perfectly like a slave. But it cannot think. The only things on earth that are capable of thinking are human beings!

How many of us use this thinking capacity?

In order to make a disciple think, the Rishis devised many methods. Many such strategies are found in Kena Upanishad. Once the thinking door is closed, we become fools. Almost like the servant in the following anecdote!

There was a trader who sold rabbits. One day, he gave a rabbit to his servant and said, "Go and deliver the rabbit to a lady and bring the cash in return, without fail. Here is the address."

The servant, while going through a crowded market place, happened to collide with a man coming in the opposite direction. He fell down and the rabbit escaped from his hand.

The servant merely stood, watching the rabbit running away. The onlookers said, "Hey, you idiot! Run and catch the rabbit!"

But the servant said unperturbed, "So what, if the rabbit ran away? Where will the rabbit go? I still have the address given by my boss safe with me!"

Do you know why I have narrated this story?

So far, I have narrated several parables only to instill the moral values of the stories in you. But, if you take only the story and keep aside the morals, you would be like the servant who was happy holding on to the address and allowing the rabbit to escape. You too would have felt content reading the stories but would not have imbibed the essential moral from them.

Ignorance is a serious curse. Being foolish is a greater punishment. The strange thing is, we are solely responsible for inflicting on ourselves both this curse this punishment.

Ramesh was a clerk in a private firm. One day, he was not feeling well. His colleagues suggested to him, "It is already 3 O'clock. Today is Saturday and the manager would not return. So why don't you simply go home?"

With a lot of hesitation and fear, Ramesh left the office. As he reached his house, he saw the manager's car parked, outside. "I could be in for trouble!" he thought, as he went stealthily behind his house. Slowly he moved a curtain aside and peeped through the window. He witnessed the ghastly sight of the manager in bed with his wife.

He ran to the office and told his colleagues, "God! Am I lucky! I was almost caught by the manager! Luckily, I escaped in time, before he noticed me!"

Now, who caught whom?

When one is foolish, look what price one has to pay for that!

In this world, it is not enough just to earn degrees from universities. One should also be intelligent.

So, read a lot! Think deeply. Work with purpose! All the twelve months of the year in your life would be like springtime!

The Guru told his disciple who was graduating from the Gurukula – (The master's house where a student spends many years studying) at the completion of his studies:

"Be like a Winnow and not like a Sieve!"

Do you know the meaning of this?

A Sieve allows all the good stuff to pass through its pores while retaining the waste materials within. A Winnow, on the other hand, blows away the stones, chaff... and retains only good grain.

What are you? A Sieve or a Winnow?

Reflections

Yoga of Wisdom

Knowledge is the ability to distinguish between the essential and unessential. Ignorance stiffens thinking and makes you lose the flexibility to see the essential and the unessential clearly.

Yoga of Action

Focus and act from what is essential. Then the mind will be wisely employed. Oh, Mind Relax Please!

Prasanna Trust is a registered social charitable trust set up with the objective to re-look at various facets of Indian philosophy and culture for effective transformation of individuals in particular and the society in general.

We have made our presence primarily through :

• Transformative Education

• Social Oriented Service

TRANSFORMATIVE EDUCATION

a) LOOKING AT LIFE DIFFERENTLY

It is a 2 days workshop on personal effectiveness through interactions and meditations. An experience oriented, non-religious program designed to enhance productivity, handling stress, personal well-being and organisational synergy. It focuses on bringing forth the outer winner leading to creativity and an inner winner to meditative consciousness.

b) EXISTENTIAL LABORATORY

It is a 4-days residential retreat set amidst natural surroundings to experience oneself through a series of dynamic and passive meditations in order to see connectivity with nature, to heal and release the inner child, to realise innocence and wonderment in all walks of life based on the Upanishad truths - Chakshumathi Vidya.

c) CORPORATE HARMONY AND CREATIVITY

It is a 2 days comprehensive workshop for senior level executives to harness creativity and harmony in today's competitive work environment and preparing them for globalisation.

d) YOUTH PROGRAMME

It is a 3 days program based on multiple intelligence. The program develops the hidden talent and skill in a child; to enable the child to face the world with confidence as each child is unique.

e) OH, MIND RELAX PLEASE!

It is a 1 day seminar based on unique techniques to transform from ordinary to extra-ordinary, dealing with fear and conflicts and converting them as challenges.

f) RELATIONSHIP SEMINAR

An exclusive workshop for couples, so as to discover intimacy and togetherness in a relationship.

g) TEACHERS' TRAINING PROGRAMME

A 5 days workshop designed to train and develop an individual as Pracharak or teacher for spreading the universal message for the benefit of society.

h) MANTRA YOGA PROGRAMME – A Holistic approach to Life

A workshop based on five powerful Mantras to help in enhancing health, unlocking the blissful centre, increasing intuitive ability, creating wealth and divinity in oneself and others. This program is conducted in English and also in many Indian languages by well trained Pracharaks.

i) NIRGUNA MANDIR – A Meditation Centre for Learning

* Unfolding the traditional texts of the Bhagavad Gita & the Upanishads as is relevant in today's living context.

* Workshops to bring forth creativity and awareness among youth, women and parents through a spiritual paradigm.

* Research to foster universal love through an inter-religious forum.

* Orientation programs for trainers and social workers.

* Spiritual inputs to deal with phobia, fear, trauma, drug and alcoholic abuse.

SOCIAL ORIENTED SERVICE

a) CHILD CARE CENTRE - A HOME FOR HOMELESS - PRASANNA JYOTHI:

Nurturing lives of little angels who have been orphaned due to the paradox of circumstances. Uncared girls who otherwise would have withered away are growing into enthusiastic, intelligent, celebrative and responsible children.

b) VOCATIONAL TRAINING FOR CHILDREN:

In order to keep abreast with the fast changing face of the world, it is proposed to give the children of Prasanna Jyothi training in office automation & allied area of skills.

We seek support of individuals, business houses, institutions and invite them to be part of this noble vision of creating an atmosphere to impart our culture and thus contributing to the society we build.

Contribution to **Prasanna Trust** account is exempted from **Income Tax under Section 80 (G)**

TITLES OF SWAMIJI'S WORKS

BOOKS

Meditation *(from Bhagavad Gita) (also in Tamil & Telugu)*

Karma Yoga *(based on Bhagavad Gita)*

Wisdom through Silence

(Commentary on Dhakshina Murthy Stotram)

Oh, Life Relax Please!

(also in Hindi, Tamil, Telugu, Gujarati and Marati)

Oh, Mind Relax Please!

(also in Tamil, Telugu, Kannada, Malayalam, Hindi, Marati & Gujarati)

Oh, Mind Relax Please! Vol. 2

(only in Tamil, Kannada & Telugu)

Looking Life Differently *(also in Tamil)*

Wordless Wisdom

Stress Management – A bullet proof Yogic Approach

Art of Wise Parenting

Agame Relax Please! *(in Tamil)*

Kutumbave Relax Please! *(in Kannada & Telugu)*

AUDIO

TRADITIONAL UNFOLDMENT

Gayatri Mantra *(also in regional languages)*

Maha Mruthyunjaya Mantra *(also in regional languages)*

Om Gam Ganapate Namaha *(also in regional languages)*

Om Krishnaya Namaha *(also in regional languages)*

Om Shivaya Namaha *(also in regional languages)*

Mantra Chants

Trataka Yogic Technique

Shiva Sutras

Essence of Bhagavad Gita

Guru Purnima

MEDITATION

Brahmayagna	Maha Visarjana Kriya
Navratri Upasana	Meditation, the Music of Silence
Bhakti Yoga	Vedic Vision to Pregnant women
Mantra Healing	Yoga Laya

OCCULT TEACHINGS

Seven Chakras of Hindu Psychology

Symbolism of Hindu Rituals

Essence of Hinduism

Who am I?

Healing Hurt through Gayatri Mantra

Handling insecurity through Mruthyunjaya Mantra

Handling crisis through Taraka Mantra

MANAGEMENT –

A NEW LOOK THROUGH SPIRITUAL PARADIGM

Self Confidence through Hypnosis

Stress Management

Art of Parenting

People Management – an enlightened approach

Creating a Happy Marriage

Hypnosis and Relationship

Living in Freedom – an Enquiry

LIFE series

VIDEO (in VCD form)

Suffering to Surrender

Jokes to Joy – Navarasa

Discouragement to Encouragement

Worry to Wisdom

Stress Management through Spirituality

Seeds of Wisdom

Looking Life Differntly

A Balanced Man

Vedanta – the dynamics of living

Inner Awakening

Harmony in Chaos

Bhagavad Gita – Chapter II (Vol. 1 & 2)

Swamiji's workshop empowers one to be
Effective, Creative & Celebrative in all walks of life.

"LIFE' - a two-days workshop on how to use the mind for Success and Satisfaction

Objective of the Seminar:

Outer Winner

◆ The art of powerful goal setting.

◆ Decision-making, Team building.

◆ Divine principles of worldly achievement.

◆ Interpersonal skills & Effective communication

◆ How to deal with difficult people.

◆ Possibility thinker.

Inner Winner

◆ The art of being blissful, restful and loving.

◆ The art of healing psychological wounds.

◆ Mind management

◆ Worry management.

◆ Fear management.

◆ Meditation to bring about healthy inner healing and enlightenment.

What others say about the programme:

"Here's one Guru who's in tune with modern times."

– India Today.

"The unusual Swami from Bangalore is the latest Guru on the Indian Management scene."

– Business India.

"He has come to be hailed as the "Corporate Guru'. The Management Swami has attempted to infuse the Corporate World with the much needed dose of ethics and spirituality."

– The Hindu.

True Freedom Lies

In the Art of Looking at Life Afresh

Glide through work pressures without the "Sting of Stress'.

Say Yes to Growth, Achievement, Progress

Say No to Stress, Fatigue, Pressure.

Oh, Mind Relax Please!
a one-day workshop

on transformation from ordinary to extra-ordinary, dealing with fear & conflicts and converting them as challenges

The programme offers:

◆ Impactful models to imbibe powerful insights, to bring forth creativity and spontaneity and discover life nourishing patterns rather than life defeating ones.

◆ Practical workouts using sciences of Pranayamas and Mudras as an antidote to the Yuppie Flu.

◆ Techniques to debug and update your inner softwares and to gracefully align to change.

◆ Processes to synergize a healthy mind with a healthy body.

For more details on Swamiji's in-house & public workshops, contact:

PRASANNA TRUST

\# 300/18, 6th Main, 14th Cross, Vyalikaval,

Bangalore – 560 003, INDIA

Telefax: (080) 2344 4112 Phone: 93437 72552

E-mail – prasannatrust@vsnl.com

prmadhav@vsnl.com

Visit us at www.swamisukhabodhananda.org

NIRGUNA MANDIR

\#1, Nirguna Mandir Layout,

Near I Block Park, Koramangala,

Bangalore – 560 047, INDIA

Phone: (080) 2552 6102

At USA

E-mail: toshakila8@hotmail.com

aruna@knology.net

parvathykancherla@yahoo.com

Please send me information on

Seminar on LIFE program

Seminar on Oh, Mind Relax Please!

Seminar on Corporate Harmony & Creativity at work

Books, Audio Cassettes, CD's, VCD's

Name.. Title.........................

Company...

Address...

City.......State..................................Pin..............................

Telephone (Off)............(Res)...

Fax.......................Email..

ABOUT THE AUTHOR

- **Swami Sukhabodhananda** is the founder Chairman of Prasanna Trust. He is also the founder of the research wing of Prasanna Foundation, which focuses on the scientific aspects of meditation.

- His several books have made many discover a new way of living life. He makes you realise that if one door closes another door opens. Life is an opening.

- He is a regular invitee to various forums in India, USA, Canada, Germany and Australia.

- He has been addressing many gatherings at important Universities in India and abroad.

- Leading industrial houses invite him to conduct "In-house workshops' for their executives.

- His self-development programs have benefited many in the corporate sectors of reputed institutions like banking, finance, industry, education, armed forces and police.

- Times of India in their recent poll on "who talks the best' places Swamiji as the one, who tops the list on all counts as the best speaker.

- The Week magazine acclaims Swamiji as one among the top five best exponent of spirituality knowledge.

- Swamiji's English books "Oh, Mind Relax Please!' and "Oh, Life Relax Please!' are the top best sellers in the country and has set a new bench mark in the lives of many... from the Kargil hero Gen. V. P. Malik who swear by the inspiring content of the book to New York Mayor who acknowledges its usefulness to diminish work pressure and dealing with New York City press!

- His other English books are marching best sellers.

- Swamiji's book "Manase Relax Please' has set an all time sales record in the history of Tamil, Kannada & Telugu books and has been included as a part of curriculum in some of the schools & colleges.

- Swamiji was invited as a dignitary in five different panels at the World Economic Forum in Davos, Switzerland and was a special invitee to the United Nation World Millennium Summit of spiritual Leaders.

- Swamiji's works in audio and video have been transforming the lives of many through Sa Re Ga Ma and Times Music.

- His message on the Astha, Gemini and many other Channels is reaching a wide spectrum of people both in India and Overseas.